GCSE
Chemistry
Revision Guide

Improving understanding through colour and clarity

Get your FREE digital book!

This book includes a free digital edition for use on computers (PC and Mac), tablets or smartphones.

**Go to ddedu.co.uk/chem
and enter this code...**

2AJW--qi-

This code is for one-time use only. It may already have been redeemed if you are not the original owner.

If you are having trouble redeeming your book code, please contact support@daydreameducation.co.uk

GCSE Chemistry

Contents

The Atom

All substances are made of atoms. An atom is the smallest part of an element that can exist.

Development of Atomic Theory

The model of the atom has changed over time as new experimental evidence has been discovered.

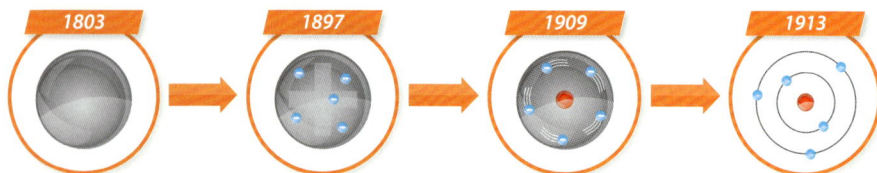

1803 **1897** **1909** **1913**

Dalton's Model
Atoms were believed to be tiny spheres that could not be divided.

Thomson's Model
After the discovery of electrons, it was proposed that atoms were balls of positive charge with embedded negative electrons. This model is known as the plum pudding model.

Rutherford's Model
Alpha particle scattering experiments found that the mass of the atom was concentrated at its centre in a positively charged nucleus.

Bohr's Model
Calculations showed that electrons orbit the nucleus in shells that are fixed distances from the nucleus.

In Rutherford's experiments, alpha particles were fired at a thin piece of gold foil. Rather than pass through the foil as expected, some particles were deflected, and some bounced back.

This proved that the plum pudding model was incorrect, so Rutherford proposed that there must be a positively charged nucleus at the centre of the atom. This model is known as the nuclear model.

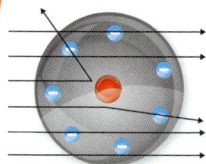

After Bohr's theory of atomic structure was accepted, further experiments by Rutherford showed evidence of smaller positively charged particles (protons) within the nucleus.

Bohr's theory was developed further by James Chadwick, who found evidence that neutral particles (neutrons) exist within the nucleus.

Chadwick made this discovery around 20 years after the nucleus had become an accepted scientific idea.

Electron Structure of Carbon: 2,4

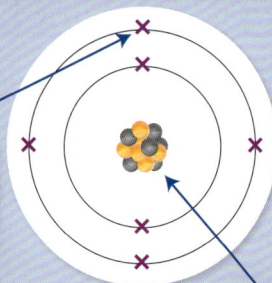

✖ Electron
⬤ Proton
🟠 Neutron

Electrons move around the nucleus in shells.

The **nucleus** contains protons and neutrons.

daydream
EDUCATION

Size & Mass of Atoms

Atoms are very small, with a radius of about 0.1 nm (1×10^{-10} m).

Although the radius of a nucleus is less than 1/10,000 of that of an atom, almost all (99.9%) of an atom's mass is in the nucleus.

If an atom were blown up to the size of a football stadium, the nucleus would be the size of a small pea on the centre circle.

The electrons would orbit the outermost edge of the stadium, but they would be far too small to be seen.

Particle Name	Proton	Neutron	Electron
Mass	1	1	Negligible

An element is a substance that contains only one type of atom and, therefore, cannot be broken down into simpler components by any non-nuclear chemical reaction.

Atoms of an element are often represented as follows:

Mass Number
This is the sum of protons and neutrons in an atom.

Atomic Number
This is the number of protons (and electrons) in an atom.

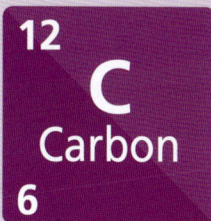

$$\begin{array}{l} 12 \\ \text{C} \\ \text{Carbon} \\ 6 \end{array}$$

Element Symbol
Elements have a one- or two-letter chemical symbol (e.g. C is the chemical symbol for carbon).

Atoms contain an equal number of protons and electrons.

The number of protons, electrons and neutrons in atoms varies. However, all atoms of a particular element have the same number of protons.

Atom	Number of Protons
Helium	2
Oxygen	8
Aluminium	13

Electronic Structure & Relative Electrical Charges of Atoms

Atoms have no electrical charge because they contain an equal number of protons and electrons.

Particle Name	Relative Charge
Proton	+1
Neutron	0
Electron	−1

- The electrons in an atom first occupy the lowest available energy levels, the shells closest to the nucleus.
- The **first shell** can hold **up to two electrons**.
- The **second and third shells** can hold **up to eight electrons**.

The electron structure of an atom can be represented by numbers or a diagram.

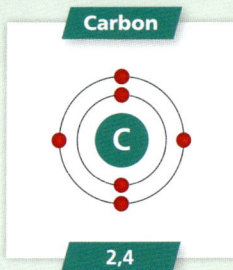

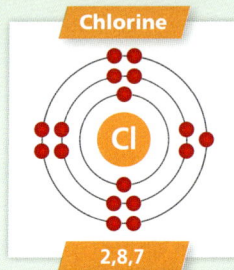

Sulfur

2,8,6

Carbon

2,4

Chlorine

2,8,7

The atomic number of an element indicates how many protons are in an atom of that element. It also represents the number of electrons. Therefore, the atomic number can be used to work out the electronic structure of the first 20 elements in the periodic table.

Example: What is the electronic structure of sodium?

1 Identify the atomic number of sodium.

The atomic number of sodium is 11, so it has 11 protons and 11 electrons.

2 Starting with the shell closest to the nucleus, occupy the shells with electrons.

Remember, the first shell can hold up to two electrons, and the second and third shells can hold up to eight.

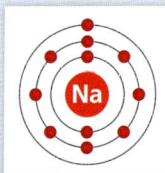

The first shell holds two electrons.

The second shell holds eight electrons.

The third shell holds one electron.

Therefore, the electronic structure is 2,8,1.

Atoms with a full outer shell of electrons are stable and unreactive.
Because sodium has only one electron in its outer shell, it is highly reactive.

daydream EDUCATION

Isotopes

Atoms of an element always have the same number of protons (and atomic number). However, they can have a different number of neutrons and, therefore, a different mass number. These are called isotopes.

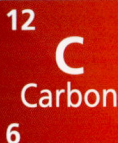

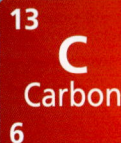

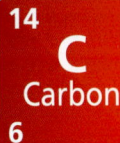

| 12 **C** Carbon 6 | 13 **C** Carbon 6 | 14 **C** Carbon 6 |

Relative Atomic Mass

The relative atomic mass (A_r) of an element is an average value of mass based on the abundance of the element's isotopes.

To calculate the relative atomic mass of an element, multiply the mass of each isotope by its abundance, add the totals together and then divide by 100:

$$A_r = \frac{(\text{Mass of isotope 1} \times \text{Abundance of isotope 1}) + (\text{Mass of isotope 2} \times \text{Abundance of isotope 2})\ldots}{100}$$

Example 1

Calculate the relative atomic mass of chlorine to one decimal place using the information provided.

25% of chlorine isotopes have a mass of 37.
75% of chlorine isotopes have a mass of 35.

$$A_r = \frac{(37 \times 25) + (35 \times 75)}{100} = 35.5$$

35.5 **Cl** Chlorine 17

The relative atomic mass of chlorine is 35.5.

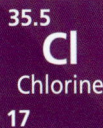

Example 2

Magnesium naturally occurs in three stable isotopes. Calculate the relative atomic mass of magnesium to one decimal place using the information provided.

79% of magnesium isotopes have a mass of 24.
10% of magnesium isotopes have a mass of 25.
11% of magnesium isotopes have a mass of 26.

$$A_r = \frac{(24 \times 79) + (25 \times 10) + (26 \times 11)}{100} = 24.3$$

24.3 **Mg** Magnesium 12

The relative atomic mass of magnesium is 24.3.

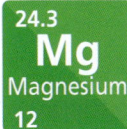

Compounds

Compounds contain two or more elements that are chemically combined.

Chemical reactions can be represented by word equations or equations using symbols and formulae.

Compounds are formed during chemical reactions.

Chemical reactions always involve the formation of one or more new substances and often involve an energy change.

The elements in the compounds are in fixed proportions and are held together by chemical bonds. Compounds can be separated back into elements only by chemical reactions.

Elements			Compound
Sodium $2Na$	+	Chlorine Cl_2	Sodium chloride $2NaCl$
Iron Fe	+	Sulfur S	Iron sulfide FeS
Hydrogen $2H_2$	+	Oxygen O_2	Water $2H_2O$

To form compounds, bonds are formed. To do this, elements gain, lose or share electrons.

Ionic Bonding

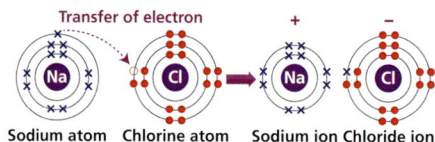

Transfer of electron

Sodium atom   Chlorine atom   Sodium ion   Chloride ion

Ionic bonding occurs in compounds formed when metal atoms react with non-metal atoms.

Electrons are transferred from the outer shell of the metal to the outer shell of the non-metal. The metal atoms lose electrons to form positive ions, and the non-metal atoms gain electrons to form negative ions.

Covalent Bonding

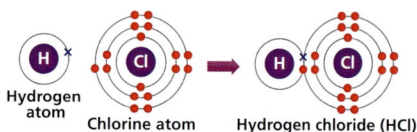

Hydrogen atom   Chlorine atom   Hydrogen chloride (HCl)

Covalent bonding occurs in most non-metallic elements and in compounds of non-metals.

In covalent bonding, pairs of electrons are shared to form molecules. The types and number of atoms in a molecule are shown in its formula.

Naming Compounds

Some basic rules apply to naming compounds.

Oxygen + Magnesium = Magnesium oxide

The metal is written first. | The non-metal comes last. Oxygen forms oxide ions.

Non-Metal Ions

The suffix -ide shows that there is only one non-metal element in the compound.

Chlorine ➡ Chloride (Cl^-)   Bromine ➡ Bromide (Br^-)

Sulfur ➡ Sulfide (S^{2-})

Non-metal ions can contain more than one element.
The suffix -ate shows that the compound contains oxygen.

Carbonate (CO_3^{2-}) | Sulfate (SO_4^{2-}) | Nitrate (NO_3^-)

daydream
EDUCATION

Chemical Equations

A chemical equation is a written representation of the process that occurs in a chemical reaction.

The white sparks from a sparkler are created when magnesium burns. Magnesium reacts with oxygen in the air to form magnesium oxide.

The word equation for this reaction is:

Magnesium + Oxygen ➡ Magnesium oxide

Word equations are a simple way of displaying a chemical reaction. However, they do not show the number of atoms involved.

Symbol Equations

During a chemical reaction, no atoms are lost or made. Therefore, the total number of atoms on each side of a chemical equation must be the same. Symbol equations show the number of atoms involved in a chemical reaction.

Reactants $2Mg + O_2$ ➡ $2MgO$ **Products**

This can also be shown as a particle diagram.

The number of oxygen and magnesium atoms is the same on both sides. The symbol equation is balanced.

State Symbols

To complete a balanced symbol equation, you can also add state symbols to show the state of each substance.

$2Mg (s) + O_2 (g)$ ➡ $2MgO (s)$

State symbols ▶ **(s) solid**   **(g) gas**   **(l) liquid**   **(aq) aqueous (a solution in water)**

Sometimes chemical formulae contain brackets. These are used when a compound contains a chemical group. For example, the chemical formula for magnesium hydroxide is $Mg(OH)_2$.

OH is a hydroxide group, and magnesium hydroxide has two of them. Therefore, the compound contains one atom of magnesium, two of oxygen and two of hydrogen.

Numbers in Chemical Equations

The chemical formula for sulfuric acid is shown below.

This number indicates the number of atoms or molecules of a substance in the reaction. It can be changed to balance an equation.

$2H_2SO_4$

These numbers indicate how many atoms of an element are in a compound. These numbers cannot be changed to balance an equation.

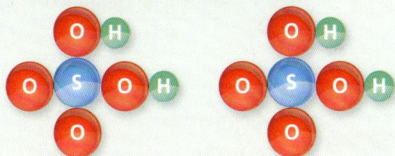

The formula shows that there are two molecules of sulfuric acid, and each one contains two hydrogen atoms, one sulfur atom and four oxygen atoms.

daydream EDUCATION

Brackets in Chemical Equations

Sometimes, brackets are used in a formula to indicate a chemical group.

This is the formula for calcium hydroxide.

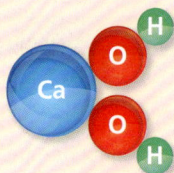

$$Ca(OH)_2$$

One atom of calcium has two hydroxide groups (–OH) attached to it. The compound contains one atom of calcium, two of oxygen and two of hydrogen. The number below the bracket cannot be changed to balance the equation.

Writing Chemical Equations

1 Write the word equation.

Hydrogen + Chlorine $\longrightarrow$ Hydrogen chloride

2 Write the symbols for each substance, including state symbols.

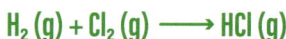

$H_2 (g) + Cl_2 (g) \longrightarrow HCl (g)$

3 Count the number of atoms of each element on both sides of the equation to determine if it is balanced.

Reactants ($H_2 + Cl_2$)		Products (HCl)	
Element	Atoms	Element	Atoms
H	2	H	1
Cl	2	Cl	1

This is not balanced. There are fewer atoms in the product.

4 If the equation is not balanced, work out how many more atoms are needed.

You need to double the number of hydrogen and chlorine atoms in the product to balance the equation.

5 Write the balanced symbol equation.

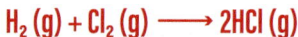

$H_2 (g) + Cl_2 (g) \longrightarrow 2HCl (g)$

Remember: You can only change the numbers in front of symbols. You cannot change the small subscript numbers.

HCl $\Longrightarrow$ 2HCl ✓   HCl $\Longrightarrow$ H_2Cl_2 ✗

Examples

Group 1 Metal and Water	Sodium $2Na (s)$	+	Water $2H_2O (l)$	$\Longrightarrow$	Sodium hydroxide $2NaOH (aq)$	+	Hydrogen $H_2 (g)$
Acid and Alkali (Neutralisation)	Hydrochloric acid $HCl (aq)$	+	Potassium hydroxide $KOH (aq)$	$\Longrightarrow$	Potassium chloride $KCl (aq)$	+	Water $H_2O (l)$
Combustion (Burning) of Methane	Methane $CH_4 (g)$	+	Oxygen $2O_2 (g)$	$\Longrightarrow$	Carbon dioxide $CO_2 (g)$	+	Water $2H_2O (l)$

daydream EDUCATION

Periodic Table

The periodic table is all of the known elements in order of atomic number. Atoms of each element are represented by a chemical symbol.

Key

9	Atomic mass
Be	Symbol
Beryllium	Name
4	Atomic number

Colour Key

- Alkali metals
- Alkaline earth metals
- Transition metals
- Other metals
- Other non-metals
- Halogens
- Noble gases
- Rare earth metals

Metals / Non-metals

Metals | Non-metals

Group 1

Period		
1	1 **H** Hydrogen 1	
2	7 **Li** Lithium 3	9 **Be** Beryllium 4
3	23 **Na** Sodium 11	24 **Mg** Magnesium 12
4	39 **K** Potassium 19	40 **Ca** Calcium 20
5	85 **Rb** Rubidium 37	88 **Sr** Strontium 38
6	133 **Cs** Caesium 55	137 **Ba** Barium 56
7	223 **Fr** Francium 87	226 **Ra** Radium 88

Group 2

Transition metals

Group 3: 45 **Sc** Scandium 21; 89 **Y** Yttrium 39; 139 **La** Lanthanum 57; 227 **Ac** Actinium 89

Group 4: 48 **Ti** Titanium 22; 91 **Zr** Zirconium 40; 178 **Hf** Hafnium 72; 261 **Rf** Rutherfordium 104

Group 5: 51 **V** Vanadium 23; 93 **Nb** Niobium 41; 181 **Ta** Tantalum 73; 262 **Db** Dubnium 105

Group 6: 52 **Cr** Chromium 24; 96 **Mo** Molybdenum 42; 184 **W** Tungsten 74; 266 **Sg** Seaborgium 106

Group 7: 55 **Mn** Manganese 25; 98 **Tc** Technetium 43; 186 **Re** Rhenium 75; 264 **Bh** Bohrium 107

56 **Fe** Iron 26; 101 **Ru** Ruthenium 44; 190 **Os** Osmium 76; 277 **Hs** Hassium 108

59 **Co** Cobalt 27; 103 **Rh** Rhodium 45; 192 **Ir** Iridium 77; 268 **Mt** Meitnerium 109

59 **Ni** Nickel 28; 106 **Pd** Palladium 46; 195 **Pt** Platinum 78; 271 **Ds** Darmstadtium 110

63.5 **Cu** Copper 29; 108 **Ag** Silver 47; 197 **Au** Gold 79; 272 **Rg** Roentgenium 111

65 **Zn** Zinc 30; 112 **Cd** Cadmium 48; 201 **Hg** Mercury 80; 285 **Cn** Copernicium 112

Group 3: 11 **B** Boron 5; 27 **Al** Aluminium 13; 70 **Ga** Gallium 31; 115 **In** Indium 49; 204 **Tl** Thallium 81; 286 **Nh** Nihonium 113

Group 4: 12 **C** Carbon 6; 28 **Si** Silicon 14; 73 **Ge** Germanium 32; 119 **Sn** Tin 50; 207 **Pb** Lead 82; 289 **Fl** Flerovium 114

Group 5: 14 **N** Nitrogen 7; 31 **P** Phosphorus 15; 75 **As** Arsenic 33; 122 **Sb** Antimony 51; 209 **Bi** Bismuth 83; 289 **Mc** Moscovium 115

Group 6: 16 **O** Oxygen 8; 32 **S** Sulfur 16; 79 **Se** Selenium 34; 128 **Te** Tellurium 52; 209 **Po** Polonium 84; 293 **Lv** Livermorium 116

Group 7: 19 **F** Fluorine 9; 35.5 **Cl** Chlorine 17; 80 **Br** Bromine 35; 127 **I** Iodine 53; 210 **At** Astatine 85; 294 **Ts** Tennessine 117

Group 0: 4 **He** Helium 2; 20 **Ne** Neon 10; 40 **Ar** Argon 18; 84 **Kr** Krypton 36; 131 **Xe** Xenon 54; 222 **Rn** Radon 86; 294 **Og** Oganesson 118

Lanthanides

140 **Ce** Cerium 58; 141 **Pr** Praseodymium 59; 144 **Nd** Neodymium 60; 145 **Pm** Promethium 61; 150 **Sm** Samarium 62; 152 **Eu** Europium 63; 157 **Gd** Gadolinium 64; 159 **Tb** Terbium 65; 162.5 **Dy** Dysprosium 66; 165 **Ho** Holmium 67; 167 **Er** Erbium 68; 169 **Tm** Thulium 69; 173 **Yb** Ytterbium 70; 175 **Lu** Lutetium 71

Actinides

232 **Th** Thorium 90; 231 **Pa** Protactinium 91; 238 **U** Uranium 92; 237 **Np** Neptunium 93; 244 **Pu** Plutonium 94; 243 **Am** Americium 95; 247 **Cm** Curium 96; 247 **Bk** Berkelium 97; 251 **Cf** Californium 98; 252 **Es** Einsteinium 99; 257 **Fm** Fermium 100; 258 **Md** Mendelevium 101; 259 **No** Nobelium 102; 260 **Lr** Lawrencium 103

Groups

The vertical columns, called groups, contain elements with similar properties. The group number indicates the number of electrons in the outer shell.

Periods

The horizontal rows, called periods, contain elements displaying a gradual change in properties. The period number indicates the number of electron shells.

Metal/Non-Metal

The bold white line on the main diagram divides metals on the left from non-metals on the right.

daydream EDUCATION

Development of the Periodic Table

Before the discovery of atomic structure, scientists attempted to classify the elements by arranging them in order of their atomic weights. However, many early tables were incomplete, and some elements were placed in unsuitable groups.

Mendeleev's Periodic Table

Today's periodic table is based on one devised by the Russian scientist Dmitri Mendeleev in 1869. Mendeleev ordered the elements according to atomic weights. However, he realised that there may be other undiscovered elements and so left gaps in his table. He also adjusted the order in consideration of the chemical properties of elements.

When he ordered the elements based on their chemical properties, they ended up in order of their atomic numbers. Mendeleev did not recognise this because protons had not been discovered yet.

Series	Group I	Group II	Group III	Group IV	Group V	Group VI	Group VII	Group VIII
1	H=1	-	-	-	-	-	-	-
2	Li=7	Be=9.4	B=11	C=12	N=14	O=16	F=19	
3	Na=23	Mg=24	Al=27.3	Si=28	P=31	S=32	Cl=35.5	-
4	K=39	Ca=40	-=44	Ti=48	V=51	Cr=52	Mn=55	Fe=56, Co=59, Ni=59, Cu=63
5	(Cu)=63	Zn=65	-=68	-=72	As=75	Se=78	Br=80	-
6	Rb=85	Sr=87	?Yt=88	Zr=90	Nb=94	Mo=96	-=100	Ru=104, Rh=104, Pd=106, Ag=108
7	(Ag)=108	Cd=112	In=113	Sn=118	Sb=122	Te=125	J=127	-
8	Cs=133	Ba=137	?Di=138	?Ce=140	-	-	-	-
9	(-)	-	-	-	-	-	-	-
10	-	-	?Er=178	?La=180	Ta=182	W=184	-	Os=195, Ir=197, Pt=198, Au=199
11	(Au)=199	Hg=200	Tl=204	Pb=207	Bi=208	-	-	-
12	-	-	-	Th=231	-	U=240	-	-

Later Modifications

Soon after Mendeleev published his table, new elements that had properties that matched the gaps in his table (e.g. gallium, scandium and germanium) were discovered.

Since the discovery of protons, the periodic table has been structured in order of atomic number rather than atomic weight. This is more accurate than atomic weight, which varies in different isotopes, because it is constant.

daydream EDUCATION

Metals and Non-Metals

Metals and Non-Metals

When atoms react, they either lose, gain or share electrons to form a full outer shell of electrons. Atoms that lose electrons form positive ions, and atoms that gain electrons form negative ions.

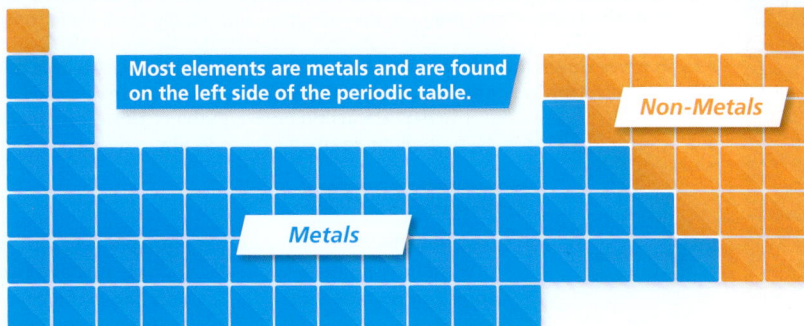

Most elements are metals and are found on the left side of the periodic table.

Non-Metals

Metals

Metals

Elements that react to form positive ions are metals. Metals have fewer electrons on their outer shell so are more likely to lose electrons and form positive ions.

Non-Metals

Elements that react to form negative ions are non-metals. Non-metals have more electrons on their outer shell so are more likely to gain electrons and form negative ions.

Non-metals that form negative ions can react with metals to form ionic compounds. Metals cannot react with other metals because positive ions repel each other.

Non-metals that do not form ions can share electrons with each other to form molecules with covalent bonds.

Properties of Metals and Non-Metals

Metals	Non-Metals
Good conductors of heat and electricity	Poor conductors of heat and electricity (except graphite, which conducts electricity)
High density	Low density
Malleable (can be hammered into shape)	Brittle (when solid)
Ductile (can be stretched into wires)	Non-ductile
High melting and boiling points (except mercury)	Low melting and boiling points
React with non-metals to form positive ions in ionic compounds	React with metals to form negative ions in ionic compounds
Do not react with other metals	React with other non-metals to form molecules
Form basic oxides	Form acidic oxides

Group 1 Elements - Alkali Metals

Group 1 – Alkali Metals

7 **Li** Lithium 3	
23 **Na** Sodium 11	
39 **K** Potassium 19	
85 **Rb** Rubidium 37	
133 **Cs** Caesium 55	
223 **Fr** Francium 87	

Increasing reactivity →

Group 1 elements are known as alkali metals. They have only one electron in their outer shell. Therefore, they are very reactive and readily form ionic compounds.

As you move down the column, the elements become more reactive. This is because the outer electron is further away from the nucleus, which means there is a weaker force of attraction between them. Therefore, melting and boiling points decrease as you move down the group.

Lithium

Potassium

Physical Properties

- Low densities*
- Low melting points*
- Form compounds that are soluble white solids

- Form positive ions with a single positive charge
- Soft and malleable
- Conduct electricity

*compared to other metals

Francium does not share these properties. It is highly unstable and breaks down as soon as it is formed.

Metal	Reaction with Water	Reaction with Chlorine	Reaction with Oxygen
All	Metal + Water = Metal hydroxide + Hydrogen	Metal + Chlorine = Metal chloride	Metal + Oxygen = Metal oxide
Lithium	Bubbles, fizzes, moves on the surface of the water and becomes smaller until it disappears	Forms lithium chloride, a white powder	Forms lithium oxide; burns with a red flame
Sodium	Bubbles, fizzes, moves on the surface of the water and melts. The hydrogen may burn with an orange flame	Reacts more vigorously than with water; produces sodium chloride, a white powder	Forms sodium oxide; burns with a yellow flame
Potassium	Bubbles, fizzes, moves on the surface of the water and melts. The hydrogen ignites, sometimes causing an explosion	Reacts violently with the chlorine to produce potassium chloride	Forms potassium oxide; burns with a lilac flame

Alkali metals are often stored in oil to stop them from reacting with oxygen and water vapour in the air.

daydream EDUCATION

Group 0 Elements – Noble Gases

Group 0 – Noble Gases

4 **He** Helium 2	
20 **Ne** Neon 10	
40 **Ar** Argon 18	
84 **Kr** Krypton 36	
131 **Xe** Xenon 54	
222 **Rn** Radon 86	

Group 0 elements have a full outer shell of electrons. Therefore, they do not need to gain or lose electrons to become more stable, and they are inert (very unreactive).

Noble gases exist as single atoms that are not bonded together, and their boiling points increase as you move down the column. This is because as molecules get bigger, the intermolecular forces between the atoms increase.

Helium

Neon

Physical Properties

- Colourless gases
- Very low melting points
- Non-metals
- Poor conductors
- Non-flammable
- Very unreactive

All elements in this group have eight electrons in their outer shell, except for helium, which has two.

In your exam, you will be expected to predict properties of the noble gases based on known trends as you move down the group.

Example

The graph below shows the boiling points of different noble gases.
Use this to estimate the boiling point of krypton.

Krypton is positioned between argon and xenon in group 0. Because the boiling points of noble gases increase as you move down the group, krypton's estimated boiling point should be midway between argon's (−186°C) and xenon's (−108°C).

$$\frac{(-186) + (-108)}{2} = \frac{-294}{2} = -147$$

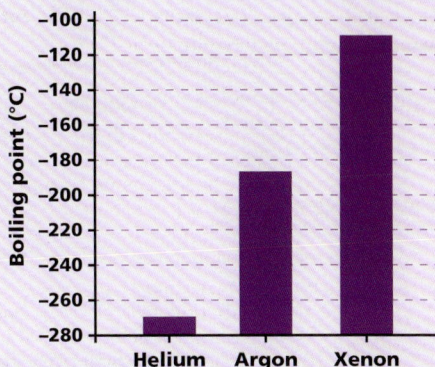

Based on the average of argon and xenon's boiling points, krypton's estimated boiling point is −147°C. Its actual boiling point is −153°C.

Group 7 Elements – Halogens

Group 7 - Halogens

19 **F** Fluorine **9**	
35.5 **Cl** Chlorine **17**	
80 **Br** Bromine **35**	
127 **I** Iodine **53**	
210 **At** Astatine **85**	

Decreasing reactivity ↓

Group 7 elements are non-metals known as halogens. They have seven electrons in their outer shell and their molecules are made up of pairs of atoms, which are joined by a single covalent bond.

As you move down the column, the elements become less reactive with higher molecular masses, melting points and boiling points. This is due to the outermost shell being increasingly further away from the nucleus, which makes it difficult to attract and gain electrons.

Fluorine

Chlorine

Physical Properties
- Low melting and boiling points
- Poor conductors
- Coloured
- Form negative ions with a single negative charge
- Toxic

At room temperature:
- Fluorine is a **yellow** gas.
- Chlorine is a **green** gas.
- Bromine is a **red-brown** liquid.
- Iodine is a **grey** crystalline solid.*

** Iodine easily vaporises to form a **purple** vapour.*

Astatine is highly radioactive and breaks down almost instantly, so its properties are uncertain.

Compounds

Halogens can share electrons via covalent bonding to form compounds with non-metals.

Hydrogen H_2 (g) **+** **Chlorine** Cl_2 (g) **➔** **Hydrogen chloride** 2HCl (g)

Halogens react with metals to form ionic compounds called halide salts.

Chlorine Cl_2 (g) **+** **Magnesium** Mg (s) **➔** **Magnesium chloride** $MgCl_2$ (s)

Displacement Reactions

A more reactive halogen can displace a less reactive halogen from a solution of its salt.

Chlorine Cl_2 (g) **+** **Sodium bromide** 2NaBr (aq) **➔** **Bromine** Br_2 (aq) **+** **Sodium chloride** 2NaCl (aq)

For example, chlorine displaces bromine from sodium bromide solution. It also displaces iodine from potassium iodide solution. However, bromine and iodine cannot displace chlorine from sodium chloride because they are less reactive.

daydream EDUCATION

Properties of Transition Metals

The transition metals, or transition elements, are found in the central part of the periodic table, between groups 2 and 3.

21 Sc	22 Ti	23 V	24 Cr	25 Mn	26 Fe	27 Co	28 Ni	29 Cu	30 Zn
39 Y	40 Zr	41 Nb	42 Mo	43 Tc	44 Ru	45 Rh	46 Pd	47 Ag	48 Cd
72 Hf	73 Ta	74 W	75 Re	76 Os	77 Ir	78 Pt	79 Au	80 Hg
104 Rf	105 Db	106 Sg	107 Bh	108 Hs	109 Mt	110 Ds	111 Rg	112 Cn

Properties

The transition metals have the same properties as all other metals, but they also have some that other metals lack.

Properties Associated with Metals

- Good conductors of heat and electricity
- High melting points (except for mercury)
- Strong
- High densities

Properties Associated with Transition Metals

- The compounds of transition metals are generally brightly coloured.
- Transition metals form positive ions with different charges (e.g. Fe^{2+} and Fe^{3+}, Cu^+ and Cu^{2+}).
- Many transition metals can act as catalysts for chemical reactions. For example, an iron catalyst is used in the Haber process to make ammonia.

Compared with the Group 1 metals, transition metals are much less reactive. They react slowly with oxygen and water and have much higher melting points. They are also stronger, harder and much denser.

Transition metals

Group 1 metals

Element	Symbol	Melting point (°C)	Density g/cm³
Chromium	Cr	1,907	7.15
Manganese	Mn	1,246	7.3
Iron	Fe	1,538	7.87
Cobalt	Co	1,495	8.86
Nickel	Ni	1,455	8.90
Copper	Cu	1,084	8.96
Lithium	Li	180	0.53
Potassium	K	63.5	0.89

daydream EDUCATION

Separating Mixtures

Key Terminology

Pure substances
Pure substances are single elements or compounds, such as water. They are not mixed with anything else and cannot be separated by physical processes.

Mixtures
Mixtures consist of two or more elements or compounds. They are not chemically combined with each other and can be separated by physical processes.

Filtration

Filtration is used to separate insoluble solids from liquids (e.g. sand from water).

- Pour the mixture into the funnel.

- Filter paper contains tiny holes that allow water, but not sand, to pass.

- Sand gathers in the filter paper.

- Water flows through the funnel and gathers in the flask.

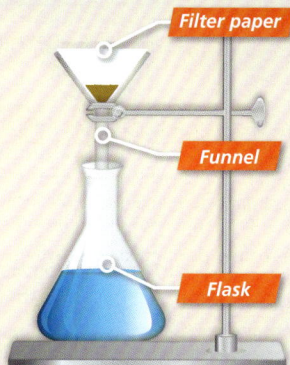

Filter paper

Funnel

Flask

Simple Distillation

Simple distillation is used to separate two liquids that have different boiling points (e.g. ethanol and water) or a solvent from a solution (e.g. water from salt).

- Heat the mixture until the substance with the lowest boiling point starts to boil and turn into a gas.

- The gas cools, condenses in the condenser and collects in the beaker. The rest of the mixture remains in the flask.

- The solution must be heated gradually so that the components of the mixture have time to evaporate at their respective boiling points.

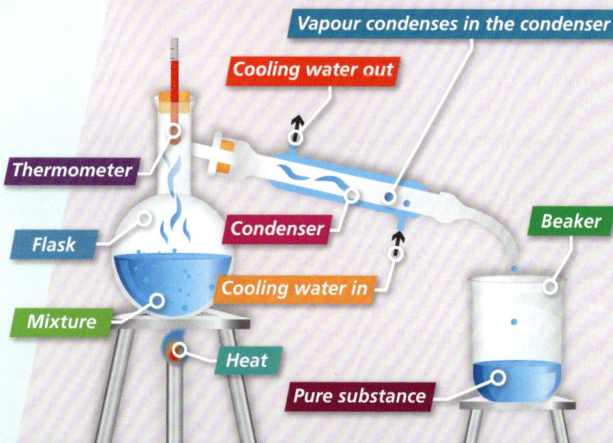

Vapour condenses in the condenser

Cooling water out

Thermometer

Flask

Condenser

Cooling water in

Mixture

Heat

Beaker

Pure substance

daydream EDUCATION

Mixtures can be separated by physical processes. The type of separating technique you choose depends on the properties of the substances in the mixture.

Evaporation and Crystallisation

Evaporation and crystallisation are used to separate solutes (dissolved substances) from solutions (e.g. a salt from its solution).

- Place the solution in an evaporating dish and gently heat.

- The solvent will start to evaporate, leaving a more concentrated solution.

- When crystals start to form, remove the dish from the heat and leave to cool.

- Once the dish has cooled, filter out the crystals (if there is any liquid remaining) and leave to dry.

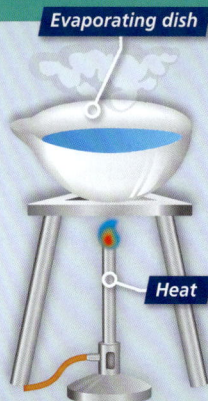

Evaporating dish

Heat

Paper Chromatography

Paper chromatography is used to separate solvents in a solution (e.g. different coloured dyes in an ink).

- Draw a line with a pencil at the bottom of a strip of paper, and add a spot of ink on the line.

- Place the paper into the solvent so the ink is above the surface of the solvent. It is important to choose a solvent that dissolves the ink.

- Place a lid on the beaker to stop the solvent from evaporating. The solvent then seeps up the paper from the bottom to the top, carrying the ink with it. The different dyes in the ink travel at different speeds so some move further than others in a given time. Therefore, each dye forms a spot in a different place on the paper.

Paper   *Lid*

Solvent

Fractional Distillation

Fractional distillation is used to separate complex mixtures (e.g. the fractions in crude oil).

- Place the solution in a flask with a fractionating column attached on top, and heat the solution.

- The solvents have different boiling points and therefore boil at different temperatures. The liquid with the lowest boiling point will boil, turn into a gas and reach the top of the column first. The column is cooler at the top. Even if liquids with higher boiling points start to boil, they will condense before reaching the top of the column and run back down to the beaker.

- Once the first liquid has been collected, increase the temperature until the next liquid reaches its boiling point.

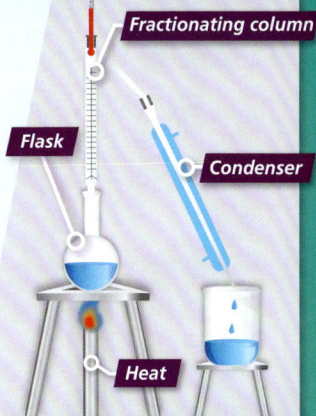

Fractionating column

Flask

Condenser

Heat

States of Matter

Particle theory is a basic model that helps to explain the properties and behaviour of materials in each of the three states. It enables us to visualise what is happening on a very small scale.

Solid

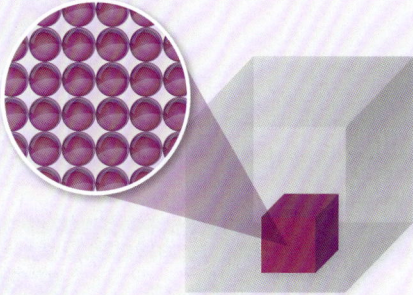

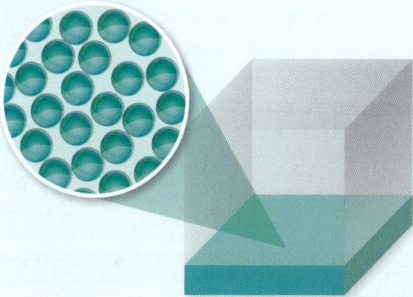

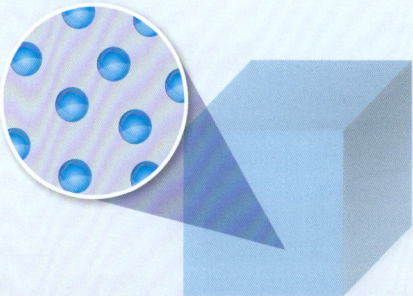

Particle Arrangement & Behaviour

- Strong forces of attraction between particles
- Usually in a regular arrangement
- Particles are close together and vibrate about fixed positions

Properties

- Has a definite shape
- Has a definite volume
- Usually has a high density
- Cannot easily be compressed

Liquid

Particle Arrangement & Behaviour

- Weak forces of attraction between particles
- Random arrangement
- Particles move about freely but are close together

Properties

- Takes the shape of its container
- Has a definite volume
- Cannot easily be compressed

Gas

Particle Arrangement & Behaviour

- Very weak forces of attraction between particles
- Random arrangement
- Particles move around freely and are far apart

Properties

- Takes the shape of its container
- Does not have a definite shape or volume
- Can easily be compressed

daydream EDUCATION

The three states of matter are solid, liquid and gas. In chemical equations, the three states of matter are shown as (s), (l) and (g) with (aq) for aqueous solutions.

Limitations

Particle theory has some limitations as a model. For example, particles are not solid spheres, and the forces between the particles are not represented in the model.

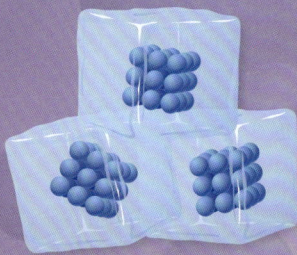 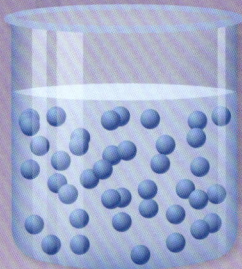 

State Changes – *Most substances can exist in all three states.*

The amount of energy needed to change state – from solid to liquid and from liquid to gas – depends on the strength of the forces between particles in a substance. The stronger the forces, the higher the melting point and boiling point of the substance.

State changes are physical changes that can be reversed. The chemical composition of the particles remains the same, but their arrangement, movement and amount of energy change.

Boiling and evaporation are both changes of state from liquid to gas. Evaporation takes place at any temperature, but boiling occurs only at the boiling point.

| Solid | Melting: when a solid changes into a liquid | Liquid | Boiling/Evaporation: when a liquid changes into a gas | Gas |

 Heat in / Heat out

 Heat in / Heat out

Ice
(10 grams)

Freezing: when a liquid changes into a solid

Water
(10 grams)

Condensation: when a gas changes into a liquid

Steam
(10 grams)

Ionic Bonding

Ions are electrically charged particles. They are formed when atoms lose or gain electrons in an attempt to gain a full outer shell of electrons.

Ionic bonding occurs in compounds formed from metals combined with non-metals. Electrons in the outer shell of metal atoms are transferred to non-metal atoms to form a more stable electronic configuration.

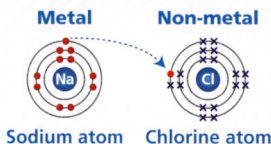

Metal

Non-metal

Sodium atom   Chlorine atom

Examples of Ionic Compounds
- Sodium chloride (NaCl)
- Magnesium oxide (MgO)
- Potassium sulfide (K_2S)

+ When metal ions form, the metal atoms lose electrons to become positively charged ions (cations).

The oppositely charged ions form ionic bonds.

When non-metal ions form, the non-metal atoms gain one or more electrons to become negatively charged ions (anions). **−**

By transferring electrons during a chemical reaction, atoms gain a full outer shell of electrons and become stable.

The charge on an ion relates to how many electrons it needs to gain or lose to have a full outer shell of electrons. The charge of the ions produced by metals in groups 1 and 2 and by non-metals in groups 6 and 7 relates to the group number of the element in the periodic table.

Group	Electrons in Outer Shell	Gain/Lose Electrons	Ions Formed	Example	
Group 1	1	Lose 1 electron	1+ ions	*Sodium*	$Na \Rightarrow Na^+ + e^-$
Group 2	2	Lose 2 electrons	2+ ions	*Magnesium*	$Mg \Rightarrow Mg^{2+} + 2e^-$
Group 6	6	Gain 2 electrons	2− ions	*Oxide*	$O + 2e^- \Rightarrow O^{2-}$
Group 7	7	Gain 1 electron	1− ions	*Chloride*	$Cl + e^- \Rightarrow Cl^-$

The ions produced by metals in groups 1 and 2 and by non-metals in groups 6 and 7 have the electronic structure of a noble gas (group 0).

Example

In this example, the sodium atom loses an electron to become a Na^+ ion, and the chlorine atom gains an electron to become a Cl^- ion.

Each atom now has eight electrons in its outer shell and becomes stable.

The oppositely charged ions are strongly attracted by electrostatic forces and form an ionic bond.

The electron transfer in ionic bonding can be represented by a dot-and-cross diagram.

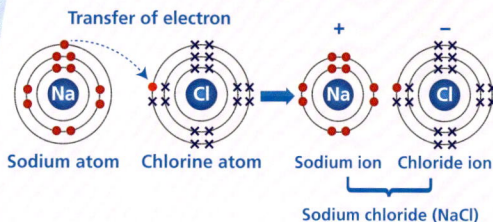

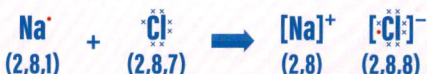

Transfer of electron

Sodium atom   Chlorine atom   Sodium ion   Chloride ion

Sodium chloride (NaCl)

$$Na^{\cdot} + \overset{\times\times}{\underset{\times\times}{\overset{\times}{Cl}}} \Rightarrow [Na]^+ \quad [\overset{\times\times}{\underset{\times\times}{\overset{\times}{Cl}}}]^-$$

(2,8,1)   (2,8,7)   (2,8)   (2,8,8)

daydream EDUCATION

Examples of Ionic Bonding

Here are some other examples of ionic bonding (with only the outer shell displayed):

Magnesium Oxide (MgO)

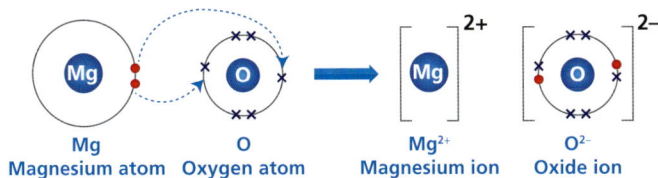

Mg	O	Mg^{2+}	O^{2-}
Magnesium atom	Oxygen atom	Magnesium ion	Oxide ion

The magnesium atom loses two electrons to become a Mg^{2+} ion, and the oxygen atom gains two electrons to become an O^{2-} ion.

Magnesium Fluoride (MgF$_2$)

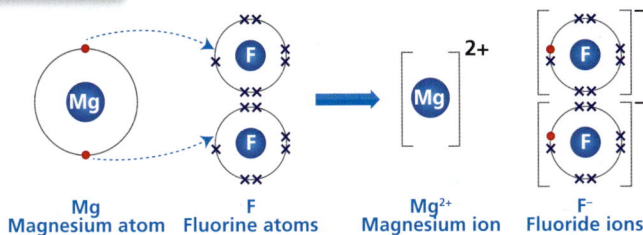

Mg	F	Mg^{2+}	F^-
Magnesium atom	Fluorine atoms	Magnesium ion	Fluoride ions

The magnesium atom loses two electrons to become a Mg^{2+} ion, and the fluorine atoms gain one electron each to become two F^- ions.

Iron Oxide (Fe$_2$O$_3$)

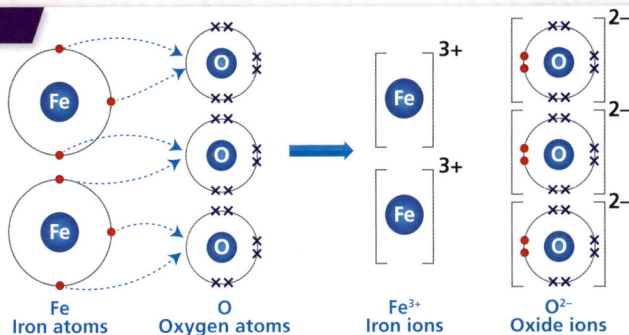

Fe	O	Fe^{3+}	O^{2-}
Iron atoms	Oxygen atoms	Iron ions	Oxide ions

The iron atoms lose three electrons to become Fe^{3+} ions, and the oxygen atoms gain two electrons each to become three O^{2-} ions.

Ionic Compounds

Ionic compounds have a giant ionic lattice structure and contain positively charged metal ions and negatively charged non-metal ions. There are strong electrostatic forces of attraction between the oppositely charged ions.

These are two ways of representing the giant ionic structure of sodium chloride:

Ball and Stick

The ball-and-stick diagram shows the arrangement of the ions. However, it is not completely accurate because the ions do not actually have gaps between them.

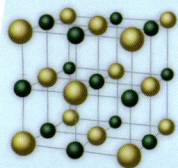

3D Model

The 3D model shows the arrangement of the ions more accurately than the ball-and-stick model, but the structure is less clear because only the outer layers can be clearly seen.

Key ● Na^+ ● Cl^-

It can be difficult to work out the formula of an ionic compound based on the above diagrams. However, it is possible to use the charges on the ions to determine the formula because the charges must balance in the formula.

Sodium Chloride

Sodium chloride is made from Na^+ and Cl^- ions. As each ion has one charge, one Na^+ is balanced by one Cl^-. The formula is NaCl.

Compound	Formula	Ions
Sodium chloride	NaCl	Na^+ Cl^-

- Sodium is found in Group 1. Its ions have a +1 charge.
- Chlorine is found in Group 7. Its ions have a –1 charge.
- The ratio of Na:Cl ions in the compound is 1:1.
- These charges are balanced, so the overall charge is neutral.

In magnesium fluoride, the magnesium ions are Mg^{2+}. So two F^- ions are needed for balance. The formula is MgF_2.

Magnesium Fluoride

- Magnesium is found in Group 2. Its ions have a +2 charge.
- Fluorine is found in Group 7. Its ions have a –1 charge.
- The ratio of Mg:F ions in the compound is 1:2.
- These charges are balanced, so the overall charge is neutral.

Compound	Formula	Ions
Magnesium fluoride	MgF_2	Mg^{2+} F^-

Properties of Ionic Compounds

High melting and boiling points	A lot of energy is needed to break the many ionic bonds in the giant lattice structure.
Brittle	If the structure of the lattice is displaced by force, similarly charged ions may align and repel each other, causing the structure to shatter.
Conduct electricity when molten or in solution	When melted or in solution, ions are free to move and therefore conduct electricity.

daydream EDUCATION

Covalent Bonding

Covalent bonding occurs in most non-metallic elements and in compounds of non-metals.

In covalent bonding, pairs of electrons are shared to form very strong bonds. The positively charged nuclei of the atoms are attracted to the negative shared electrons.

By sharing electrons, atoms gain a full outer shell of electrons and become stable.

Examples of Covalent Compounds
- Hydrogen chloride (HCl)
- Water (H_2O)
- Diamond
- Polymers

The sharing of electrons in covalent bonding can be represented by a dot-and-cross diagram.

In this example, both the hydrogen and chlorine atoms need one electron to become stable (i.e. to have a full outer shell of electrons).

Therefore, the hydrogen and chlorine atoms share a pair of electrons in their outer shell.

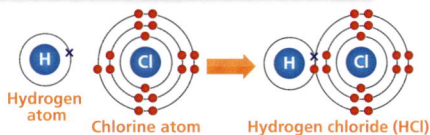

Hydrogen atom   Chlorine atom   Hydrogen chloride (HCl)

Covalent bonding can also be represented in other ways. Look at how ammonia (NH_3) is represented:

Molecules are formed through covalent bonding. The electron arrangement of some simple molecules joined by covalent bonds are shown below.

Hydrogen

Hydrogen atoms have only one electron, so two hydrogen atoms share a pair of electrons in a single bond to form a hydrogen molecule (H_2).

Chlorine

Chlorine atoms need one electron to gain a full outer shell, so two chlorine atoms share a pair of electrons in a single bond to form a chlorine molecule (Cl_2).

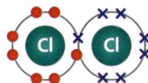

Nitrogen

Nitrogen atoms need three electrons to gain a full outer shell, so two nitrogen atoms share three pairs of electrons in a triple bond to form a nitrogen molecule (N_2).

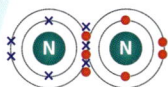

Oxygen

Oxygen atoms need two electrons to gain a full outer shell, so two oxygen atoms share two pairs of electrons in a double bond to form an oxygen molecule (O_2).

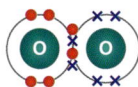

Methane

A carbon atom forms four bonds with four hydrogen atoms to form a methane molecule (CH_4).

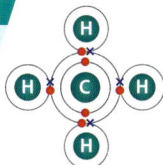

Water

An oxygen molecule forms two bonds with two hydrogen atoms to form a water molecule (H_2O).

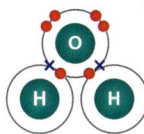

daydream EDUCATION

Covalent Compounds

Carbon Monoxide (CO)

(*Mono-* means one.)

Carbon Dioxide (CO₂)

(*Di-* means two.)

Water (H₂O)

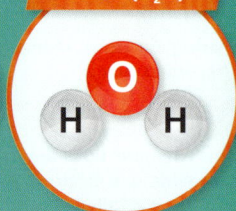

Hydrogen Chloride (HCl)

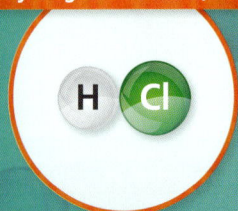

Methane (CH₄)

Ammonia (NH₃)

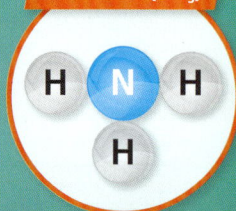

Many covalent compounds have small molecules that are gases or liquids at room temperature.

Properties of Small Molecules

Although there are strong covalent bonds between the atoms in small molecules, the intermolecular forces are weak. Therefore, they have relatively low melting points and boiling points and are easy to separate.

Intermolecular forces increase with the size of molecules, so larger molecules have higher melting and boiling points.

Because the atoms in small molecules are joined by covalent bonds, they do not have an electrical charge. There are no free electrons to carry a charge, so they do not conduct electricity.

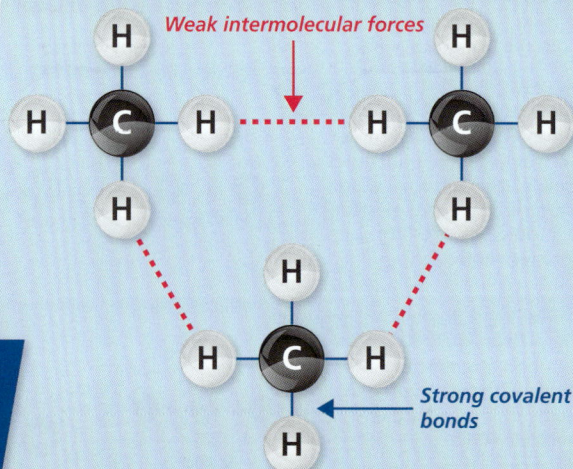

Weak intermolecular forces

Strong covalent bonds

daydream EDUCATION

Polymers & Giant Covalent Structures

Polymers and giant covalent structures are joined together by covalent bonds.

Polymers

A polymer is a very large molecule made from smaller molecules or atoms, called monomers, linked by covalent bonds. They have relatively strong intermolecular forces so are solids at room temperature.

The polymer poly(ethene) is made up of lots of ethene monomers.

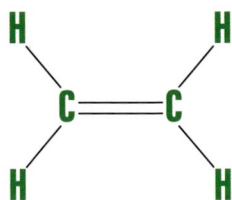

Ethene

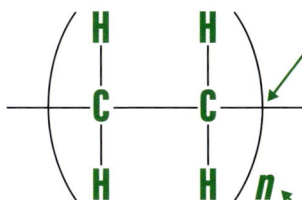

Poly(ethene)

The bond where the monomers join together

The number of times the unit is repeated

Notice that the carbon atoms in the monomer have a double covalent bond but only a single covalent bond in the polymer.

Giant Covalent Structures

In a giant covalent structure, all the atoms are linked to other atoms by strong covalent bonds. A huge amount of energy is required to break the bonds. Therefore, these structures are solids with very high melting and boiling points.

Diamond

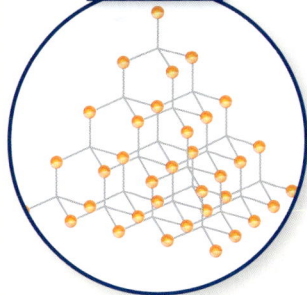

Graphite

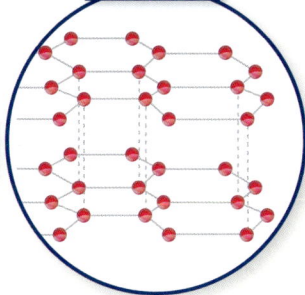

Silicon Dioxide (Silica)

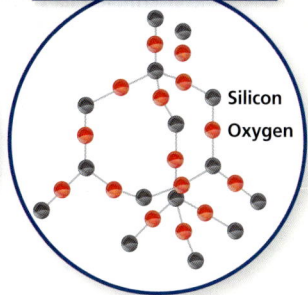

Silicon
Oxygen

Both diamond and graphite are made from carbon atoms.

Most substances that have giant covalent structures do not conduct electricity in any state because they have no free electrons or ions to carry charge (graphite is an exception).

Forms of Carbon

Diamond, graphite, graphene and fullerenes are examples of giant covalent structures that are made of only carbon atoms. Their properties relate to their structure.

Diamond

In diamond, each carbon atom forms four covalent bonds with other carbon atoms.

Because of its hardness, diamond is often used to strengthen cutting tools.

Properties	Relation to Structure
Very hard	Diamond has a rigid lattice structure, with strong bonds that are hard to break.
High melting point	A lot of energy is needed to break the strong covalent bonds.
Does not conduct electricity	All the outer electrons are used in the covalent bonds and are not free to move.

Graphite

In graphite, each carbon atom forms three covalent bonds with other carbon atoms. The atoms form layers of hexagonal rings that are held together by weak forces. Each carbon atom has one delocalised electron that is free to move around.

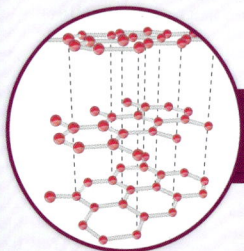

Graphite is often used as a lubricant because of its slipperiness. It is also used in electrodes because of its electrical conductivity.

Properties	Relation to Structure
Soft and slippery	Weak forces between the layers allow them to break and slide over each other.
High melting point	A lot of energy is needed to break all the bonds.
Conducts electricity	The delocalised electrons are free to move.

daydream EDUCATION

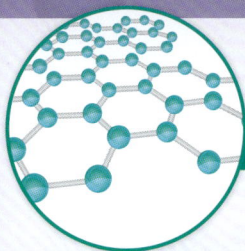

Graphene is a single layer of graphite.

Properties	Use Based on This Property	Relation to Structure
Very strong	Makes composite materials stronger	Strong covalent bonds exist between all atoms.
Transparent	Touchscreen devices	It is only one atom thick.
Conducts electricity	Electronics	Delocalised electrons are free to move.

Fullerenes

Fullerenes are molecules of carbon atoms with hollow shapes such as spheres and tubes. They are mainly composed of hexagonal rings of carbon atoms but can also contain rings with five or seven carbon atoms.

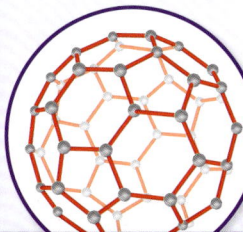

This was the first fullerene to be discovered.

Cylindrical fullerenes have very high length-to-diameter ratios.

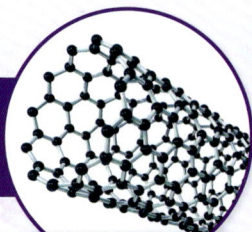

Buckminsterfullerene (C_{60})

Carbon nanotube

Properties	Use Based on This Property
Hollow shape	Carries drug molecules around the body
High tensile strength	Reinforces materials (e.g. in tennis rackets)
High electrical conductivity	Used as a semiconductor in electrical circuits
Large surface area	Helps make catalysts

Metallic Bonding & Properties of Metals & Alloys

Metallic Bonding

Metallic bonding occurs in metallic elements and alloys.

Metals consist of closely packed, positively charged metal ions arranged in a regular pattern and a 'sea' of negatively charged, delocalised electrons.

The electrons in the outer shell of the metal atoms are free to move through the whole structure.

The electrostatic forces between these electrons and the metal ions give rise to strong metallic bonds.

Examples of Metals

- Iron
- Copper
- Steel
- Bronze

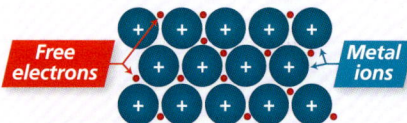

Free electrons *Metal ions*

The bonding in metals can be represented in the following forms:

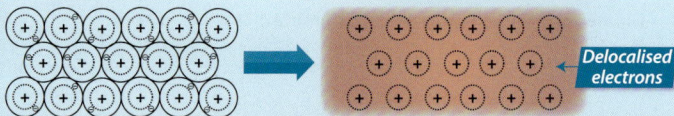

Delocalised electrons

The Properties of Metals & Alloys

The strong metallic bonds between the atoms in metals usually give them high melting and boiling points (mercury is an exception).

Metals are generally good conductors of electricity due to the ability of their delocalised electrons to move and carry electrical charge through the substance. They can also collide and transfer energy, so they are good conductors of heat.

Force

It is relatively easy to distort metals as the layers of atoms can slide over each other whilst still maintaining their bond. Therefore, most metals are malleable (can be bent and shaped).

This property means that pure metals are too soft for many uses and therefore are mixed with other elements, mainly metals, to make harder alloys.

Alloys

An alloy is a mixture of elements, usually metals. They have metallic bonds, but due to the different sizes of the atoms, the layers are distorted, which makes the substance much harder and more difficult to shape.

Brass
(copper and zinc)

Stainless Steel
(iron, carbon and a minimum of 10.5% chromium)

High Speed Steel
(various elements including carbon, tungsten and chromium)

daydream EDUCATION

Nanoparticles

Bulk & Surface Properties of Matter

The size of particles can affect their properties. Extremely small particles called nanoparticles, have some unusual and useful properties.

Particle Size

Nanoscience is the study of nanoparticles, which are roughly the size of a few hundred atoms, regardless of atom size. Chemists classify particles into three groups based on size.

Nanoparticles
Diameter = 1 – 100 nm
(1×10^{-9} m – 1×10^{-7} m)

Fine Particles (PM$_{2.5}$)
Diameter: 100 – 2,500 nm
(1×10^{-7} m – 2.5×10^{-6} m)

Coarse Particles (Dust) (PM$_{10}$)
Diameter 2,500 – 10,000 nm
(2.5×10^{-6} m – 1×10^{-5} m)

$$1 \text{ nm} = 1 \times 10^{-9} \text{ m} = 0.000,000,001 \text{ m}$$

Where a substance exists as nanoparticles, its properties differ from when it is in larger particles because of the nanoparticles' high surface area-to-volume ratio.

$$\text{Surface area-to-volume ratio} = \frac{\text{Surface area}}{\text{Volume}}$$

Look at these shapes.

Although the total volumes of A and B are the same, B is made up of multiple small cubes. Therefore, B has a much larger surface area and surface area-to-volume ratio than A.

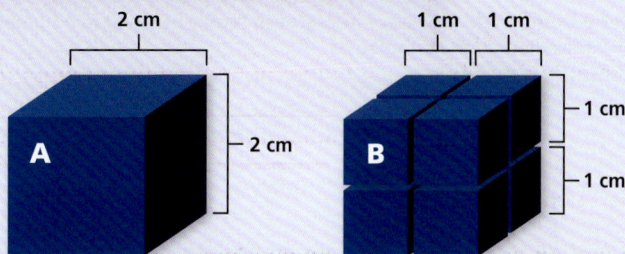

Figure	No. of Cubes	Dimensions (cm)	Surface Area (cm²)	Volume (cm³)	Ratio
A	1	2 × 2	2 × 2 × 6 = 24	2 × 2 × 2 = 8	3 : 1
B	8	1 × 1	8 (1 × 1 × 6) = 48	8 (1 × 1 × 1) = 8	6 : 1

As the length of the side of a cube decreases by a factor of 10, its surface area-to-volume ratio increases by a factor of 10. Nanoparticles are not cubes, but the principle applies.

Nanoparticles' large surface area-to-volume ratio enables them to be more effective in smaller quantities than larger particles.

Uses of Nanoparticles

Nanoscience is relatively new, so research into possible applications for nanoparticulate materials is ongoing.

Cosmetics

Nanoparticles are used in deodorants and sun creams because small particles can penetrate deeper into the skin than larger particles.

The nanoparticles in sun cream are so small that they do not reflect light. This makes them invisible, so the sun cream is undetectable on the skin.

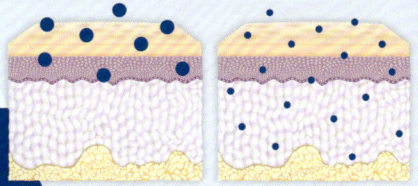

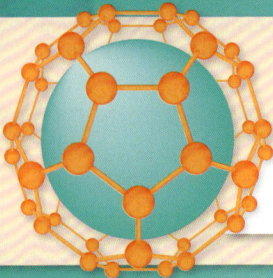

Medicine

Nanocages are used to deliver drugs to specific sites in the body. Formed from nanoparticles, they encase drugs for delivery.

A nanocage enclosing a drug

Also, silver nanoparticles are used in dressings. Silver protects against bacteria, and silver nanoparticles have enhanced antibacterial properties compared to normal particles.

Electronics

Nanowires are incredibly small wires that have helped reduce the size of various products. They have also proved highly efficient in a number of complex electronic technologies.

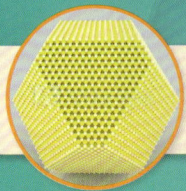

Catalysts

Catalysts rely on their surface properties. Because nanoparticles have a huge surface area, they are very efficient catalysts.

Concerns About Nanoparticles

- Nanoparticles have properties that differ from those of larger particles, and they may have as-yet-unknown properties that could be harmful.
- Nanoparticles are so small they can enter living cells. It is unknown whether this could result in harm to cells.
- It is virtually impossible to stop the spread of nanoparticles in the environment.

Concerns about nanoparticles stem from a lack of knowledge, not from evidence of harm. Further research should establish whether these health and environmental concerns are valid.

daydream
EDUCATION

Relative Formula Mass & Conservation of Mass

Relative Formula Mass

The relative formula mass (M_r) of a compound is the sum of the relative atomic masses (A_r) of the atoms in the compound. Remember, relative atomic mass is the average mass of atoms of an element based on the abundance of each isotope that exists.

In a balanced chemical equation, the sum of the relative formula masses of the reactants must equal the sum of the relative formula masses of the products.

Compound	Formula	A_r of Atoms	M_r
Carbon dioxide	CO_2	C = 12, O = 16	$12 + (2 \times 16) = 44$
Iron chloride	$FeCl_3$	Fe = 55.8, Cl = 35.5	$55.8 + (3 \times 35.5) = 162.3$
Calcium sulfate	$CaSO_4$	Ca = 40, S = 32, O = 16	$40 + 32 + (4 \times 16) = 136$
Magnesium nitrate	$Mg(NO_3)_2$	Mg = 24, N = 14, O = 16	$24 + (2 \times 14) + (6 \times 16) = 148$

Conservation of Mass & Balancing Chemical Equations

During a chemical reaction, no atoms are made or lost, so the mass of the products will always equal the mass of the reactants. This is known as conservation of mass. It also means that there are the same type and number of atoms before and after a chemical reaction has taken place.

Symbol equations show the number of atoms involved in a chemical reaction.

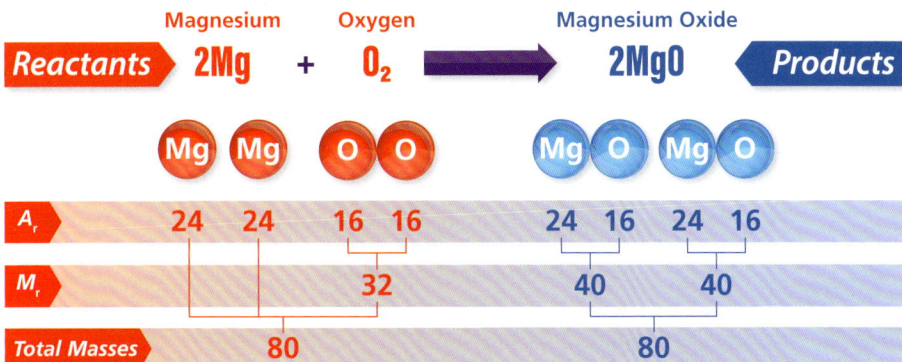

	Magnesium	Oxygen		Magnesium Oxide	
Reactants	$2Mg$	$+$ O_2	→	$2MgO$	**Products**

A_r	24 24	16 16		24 16	24 16
M_r		32		40	40
Total Masses	80			80	

The number of oxygen and magnesium atoms is the same on both sides, so the equation is balanced. The total masses on both sides of the equation must also balance.

daydream EDUCATION

When Mass Appears to Change

The law of conservation of mass indicates that the mass of the products must always equal the mass of the reactants. However, reactions often seem to involve a change in mass. This is usually because a reactant or product is a gas, and its mass has not been included.

Copper reacts with oxygen to form copper oxide.

The mass of copper oxide will be greater than that of the copper because oxygen has been added to it.

$$2Cu + O_2 \longrightarrow 2CuO$$

Calcium carbonate is broken down by heat to form calcium oxide and carbon dioxide.

The mass of calcium oxide is less than that of the calcium carbonate because mass has been lost from the system as carbon dioxide.

$$CaCO_3 \longrightarrow CaO + CO_2$$

Measurements and Uncertainty

Scientific results hardly ever turn out exactly the same when you repeat measurements. This can be due to random error or limits to the resolution of the instruments used. Every measurement you make has a level of uncertainty. How big this uncertainty is varies depending on the situation.

The resolution of an instrument is the smallest change it can detect.

Calculating the Uncertainty of Mean Results

The uncertainty of a mean can be calculated from the range using this formula:

$$uncertainty = \frac{range}{2}$$

Uncertainty can be reduced by doing more repeats or samples. The greater the uncertainty, the less confidence you can have in the accuracy of your results.

Precision relates to the range of the results. Results with a small range are called precise.

Moles

Chemical amounts are measured in moles. The symbol for the unit mole is mol.

A mole of a substance is a mass, and it varies from one substance to another. It is the relative formula mass (M_r) in grams. Moles can apply to atoms, molecules, ions and electrons.

The M_r of potassium (K) is 39 so 1 mole of potassium is 39 g.

The M_r of nitrogen (N_2) is 28 so 1 mole of nitrogen is 28 g.

The M_r of sulfuric acid (H_2SO_4) is 98 so 1 mole of sulfuric acid is 98 g.

Remember, M_r is an average mass for all the isotopes of an element.

The Avogadro Constant

One mole of any given substance will always contain the same number of particles (atoms, molecules or ions, depending on the substance) as one mole of any other substance. That number is called the Avogadro constant, and its value is 6.02×10^{23}.

For example, 1 mole of carbon (an atom) contains the same number of atoms as there are molecules in 1 mole of carbon dioxide (a molecule):

$$6.02 \times 10^{23}$$

Calculating the Number of Moles in a Given Mass

The number of moles in a given mass can be calculated using the following equation:

$$\text{Number of moles} = \frac{\text{mass (grams (g))}}{M_r \text{ (moles (mol))}}$$

How many moles are there in 32 g of sulfur dioxide (SO_2)?

$$\text{number of moles} = \frac{\text{mass}}{M_r}$$

$$M_r = 32 + (2 \times 16) = 64$$

$$\text{number of moles} = \frac{32}{64}$$

$$= 0.5 \text{ mol}$$

Calculate the mass of 10 moles of carbon dioxide (CO_2).

$$\text{mass} = \text{number of moles} \times M_r$$

$$\text{mass} = 10 \times 44$$

$$= 440 \text{ g}$$

$$M_r = 12 + (2 \times 16) = 44$$

Moles in Equations

The masses of reactants and products can be calculated using balanced equations.

$$Mg + 2HCl \longrightarrow MgCl_2 + H_2$$

This equation shows that one mole of magnesium reacts with two moles of hydrochloric acid to form one mole of magnesium chloride and one mole of hydrogen.

Relative atomic masses: $Mg = 24$ $Cl = 35.5$ $H = 1$

Using the relative atomic masses of the elements involved, we can calculate that:

24 g of magnesium (1 mole) will react with 73 g of hydrochloric acid (2 moles) to form 95 g of magnesium chloride (1 mole) and 2 g of hydrogen (1 mole).

Mg	+	$2HCl$		$MgCl_2$	+	H_2
24	+	$(2 \times 1) + (2 \times 35.5)$		$24 + (35.5 \times 2)$	+	(1×2)
24	+	73		95	+	2

Calculating the Mass of a Product from the Mass of a Reactant

Using the same equation, we can calculate how much magnesium chloride will be produced if we use a given mass of hydrochloric acid by converting the mass into moles.

What mass of magnesium chloride is produced when 50 g of hydrochloric acid is mixed with magnesium?

1	Calculate the mass of 1 mole of HCl.	$1 + 35.5 = 36.5$ g
2	Calculate the number of moles in 50 g of HCl.	number of moles $= \dfrac{50}{36.5} = 1.37$ mol
3	Each mole of HCl produces 0.5 mol of $MgCl_2$.	2 mol of HCl produce 1 mol of $MgCl_2$, so 1 mol will produce 0.5 mol.
4	Calculate how much $MgCl_2$ will be produced by 1.37 moles of HCl.	$0.5 \times 1.37 = 0.685$ mol
5	Calculate the mass of 1 mole of $MgCl_2$.	$24 + 35.5 + 35.5 = 95$ g
6	Calculate the mass of 0.685 mol of $MgCl_2$.	$0.685 \times 95 = 65.08$ g

Assuming that there is enough magnesium for the hydrochloric acid to react with, 50 g of HCl will produce 65.08 g of $MgCl_2$.

We can use the same method in reverse to calculate how much of a reactant will be needed to produce a given mass of product.

$$2Mg \quad + \quad O_2 \quad \longrightarrow \quad 2MgO$$

Calculate the mass of oxygen needed to form 20 g of magnesium oxide.

1	Calculate the mass of 1 mole of MgO.	$24 + 16 = 40$ g
2	Calculate the number of moles in 20 g of MgO.	number of moles $= \dfrac{20}{40} = 0.5$ mol
3	Each mole of O_2 produces 2 moles of MgO.	
4	Calculate how many moles of O_2 will be needed to produce 0.5 mol of MgO.	$0.5 \div 2 = 0.25$ mol
5	Calculate the mass of 1 mole of O_2.	$16 + 16 = 32$ g
6	Calculate the mass of 0.25 mol of O_2.	$32 \times 0.25 = 8$ g

Assuming that there is enough magnesium for the oxygen to react with, 20 g of MgO will be produced by 8 g of O_2.

daydream
EDUCATION

Using Moles to Balance Equations

The balancing numbers in a symbol equation can be calculated from the masses of reactants and products. The masses (in grams) are converted to moles, and then the numbers of moles are converted into simple whole number ratios.

This is the reverse process of calculating masses of reactants and products from an equation.

Example

6 g of magnesium reacts with 18.25 g of hydrochloric acid to produce 23.75 g of magnesium chloride and 0.5 g of hydrogen.

1	Calculate the moles for each substance.	**Mg:** no. of moles = $\dfrac{6}{24}$ = 0.25 mol	**HCl:** no. of moles = $\dfrac{18.25}{36.5}$ = 0.5 mol
		MgCl$_2$: no. of moles = $\dfrac{23.75}{95}$ = 0.25 mol	**H:** no. of moles = $\dfrac{0.5}{2}$ = 0.25 mol

2	Calculate the simplest whole number ratios for the substances in the reaction.	The ratio of the chemicals is: 0.25 Mg : 0.5 HCl : 0.25 MgCl$_2$: 0.25 H$_2$ The ratio whole numbers are: 1 Mg : 2 HCl : 1 MgCl$_2$: 1 H$_2$

3	Therefore the equation is:	**Mg** + **2HCl** $\longrightarrow$ **MgCl$_2$** + **H$_2$**

Limiting Reactants

In a chemical reaction involving two reactants, it is common to use an excess of one of the reactants so that all the other reactant is used. The reactant that is completely consumed is called the limiting reactant because it is the one that limits the amount of the products.

Calculating the Concentration of Solutions

The concentration of a solution can be measured by calculating the mass of the solute per given volume of solution, often in grams per cubic decimetre (g/dm^3).

$$concentration = \frac{mass\ of\ solute}{volume}$$

Often you will need to covert the volume from cm^3 to dm^3 (1 dm^3 = 1,000 cm^3).

1	A student adds 10 g of sodium carbonate to 300 cm^3 of water. What is the concentration of the solution obtained?	300 cm^3 = 0.3 dm^3 concentration = $\dfrac{10}{0.3}$ = 33.3 g The concentration is 33.3 g/dm^3.
2	A solution of sodium chloride has a concentration of 70 g/dm^3. What mass of sodium chloride is in 200 cm^3 of this solution?	70 g/dm^3 = $\dfrac{mass}{0.2}$ mass = 70 × 0.2 = 14 g The solution has 14 g of sodium chloride.

daydream
EDUCATION

Yield & Atom Economy of Chemical Reactions

It is possible to calculate the mass of a product that can be produced (the yield) when using a given mass of reactants. However, this yield is theoretical. It cannot be achieved because no chemical reaction is 100% efficient. Several factors can contribute to this:

- Some product may be left behind after transfers. For example, when a solution is poured from a beaker into an evaporating dish, some solution remains on the sides of the beaker.

- If a reaction is reversible, it cannot go to completion. For example, ammonium chloride breaks down when heated to form ammonia and hydrogen chloride. As the ammonia and hydrogen chloride build up, their increasing concentrations favour the reverse reaction, which prevents all the ammonium chloride from being used up.

- One reactant may be limiting, meaning there is not enough of it to consume all the other reactant completely.

- The product may react with another chemical (e.g. oxygen in the air).

Percentage Yield

To maximise the yield of a reaction, first determine how efficient a chemical process is by calculating the **percentage yield**.

$$\text{Percentage yield} = \frac{\text{Mass of product actually made}}{\text{Maximum theoretical mass of a product}} \times 100$$

Example

The maximum amount of magnesium chloride that could be produced from 50g of magnesium is 65.08g. This is the theoretical yield.

Suppose that this reaction is performed with 50 g of magnesium, but it yields only 45.6 g of magnesium chloride. The percentage yield would be:

$$Mg + 2HCl \longrightarrow MgCl_2 + H_2$$

$$\text{Percentage yield} = \frac{45.6}{65.08} \times 100$$

$$= 70$$

The percentage yield is 70%.

Why Percentage Yield Is Useful

- In commercial reactions, maximising yield is important. Reactants cost money, so inefficient reactions can be costly. Also, if a yield is to be sold, inefficiencies can reduce profit.

- Increasing the efficiency of commercial reactions makes them more sustainable, reduces waste and conserves resources and energy. It may reduce pollution as well.

daydream
EDUCATION

Atom Economy

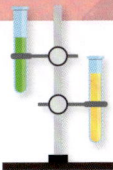

Atom economy is another way to determine the efficiency of reactions.

It is a measure of the amount of starting materials that end up as useful products. It is calculated by using the following equation:

$$\text{Percentage atom economy} = \frac{\text{Relative formula mass of desired product}}{\text{Relative formula mass of all reactants}} \times 100$$

Example

In the brewing industry, ethanol (alcohol), the desired product, is made by fermenting glucose. This process also forms a waste product, carbon dioxide. Calculate the relative formula masses (M_r) of ethanol and glucose, the only reactant.

$$C_6H_{12}O_6 \implies 2C_2H_5OH + 2CO_2$$

Calculate the relative formula masses of glucose (the only reactant) and ethanol (the desired product).

Compound	Formula	Relative Atomic Mass	M_r
Glucose	$C_6H_{12}O_6$	C = 12, H = 1, O = 16	$(12 \times 6) + (1 \times 12) + (16 \times 6) = 180$
Ethanol	C_2H_5OH	C = 12, H = 1, O = 16	$(12 \times 2) + (1 \times 6) + (16 \times 1) = 46$

The formula indicates there are two ethanol molecules, each with an M_r of 46. Therefore, the total M_r is 92.

In this reaction there is only one reactant. However, some reactions involve more than one reactant. In such cases, the M_r of all reactants must be added together.

$$\text{Percentage atom economy} = \frac{92}{180} \times 100$$

$$= 51.1$$

The percentage atom economy is 51.1%.

This means that 48.9% of the glucose does not end up as alcohol and is considered 'wasted'. However, in brewing, there is no alternative reaction to glucose fermentation.

When multiple reactions can form the desired product, their percentage atom economies can be used to compare their efficiencies. The one with the highest percentage atom economy will produce the least waste and use resources most efficiently.

Concentrations of Solutions in mol/dm³

Concentrations of solutions are expressed in g/cm³, but chemists more frequently use mol/dm³. Remember that one mole (mol) of a substance is its relative formula mass (M_r) in grams.

Using Mass to Determine Concentration

We can find the concentration of a solution by converting its mass into moles and then calculating how many moles would be present in 1 dm³.

5 g of potassium chloride is added to 250 cm³ of water. Calculate the concentration of the solution?

The formula of potassium chloride is KCl.

The relative atomic mass (A_r) of potassium is 39. The A_r of chlorine is 35.5. Therefore, the M_r of potassium chloride = 39 + 35.5 = 74.5

1 Calculate the mass of KCl that would be present in 1 dm³ (1,000 cm³) of solution.

250 cm³ (0.250 dm³) of solution contains 5 g of KCl, so 1 dm³ of solution will contain:

$$5 \times \frac{1000}{250} = 20 \text{ g}$$

2 Calculate how many moles of KCl 20 g represents.

1 mole of KCl = 74.5 g

$$20 \text{ g} = \frac{20}{74.5} = 0.27 \text{ moles}$$

The concentration of the solution is 0.27 mol/dm³

Determining the Mass of Solute in a Given Volume of Solution

If the concentration of a solution in mol/dm³ is known, it is possible to calculate the mass of the solute in the given volume of the solution.

The concentration of a solution of sodium nitrate is 2 mol/dm³. How much sodium nitrate will be present in 150 cm³?

The formula of sodium nitrate is $NaNO_3$.

The A_r of sodium is 23. The A_r of nitrogen is 14. The A_r of oxygen is 16. Therefore, the M_r of sodium nitrate is 23 + 14 + (16 × 3) = 85

1 Calculate the mass of $NaNO_3$ in the solution.

A 1 mol/dm³ solution contains 85 g $NaNO_3$. Therefore, a 2 mol/dm³ solution contains 85 × 2 = 170 g $NaNO_3$.

2 Calculate the mass of sodium nitrate in 150 cm³.

170 × 0.15 = 25.5 g $NaNO_3$

Determining the Moles of Solute in a Given Volume of Solution

If the concentration of a solution in mol/dm³ is known, it is easy to calculate the number of moles in any given volume of the solution.

The concentration of a solution of ammonium carbonate is 0.5 mol/dm³. How many moles are present in 125 cm³ of this solution?

1 dm³ = 1000 cm³

Therefore, in 125 cm³ of solution, there will be 0.5 × 0.125 = **0.06 moles** (2 d.p.)

daydream EDUCATION

Volumes of Gases & Amount of Substances

At the same temperature and pressure, one mole of a gas will occupy the same volume as one mole of any other gas. At room temperature and pressure (taken to be 20°C and 1 atmosphere pressure) **one mole of gas occupies 24 dm³.**

Using this data, the volume of a gas at room temperature and pressure (rtp) can be calculated from its mass and relative formula mass:

Cubic decimetres (dm³) →

grams (g)

$$\text{volume of gas} = \frac{\text{mass of gas}}{M_r \text{ of gas}} \times 24$$

What is the volume of 1.5 g of oxygen at room temperature and pressure?

The formula of oxygen is O_2.

The M_r of oxygen gas is $16 \times 2 = 32$

Therefore, 1 mole of oxygen gas is 32 g

$$\text{volume of oxygen} = \frac{\text{mass}}{M_r} \times 24$$

$$= \frac{1.5}{32} \times 24$$

$$= 0.046875 \times 24$$

$$= 1.125$$

Therefore, 0.047 mol will occupy 1.125 dm³

Calculating Volumes of Gases in Equations

Hydrogen and chlorine react to form hydrogen chloride gas. The equation below shows that 1 mol of hydrogen reacts with 1 mol of chlorine to form 2 mols of hydrogen chloride.

$$H_2(g) \quad + \quad Cl_2(g) \quad \longrightarrow \quad 2HCl(g)$$

A mole of any gas occupies the same volume, so the ratio of the volumes of gases will be the same as the ratio of the moles. In this case, a given volume of hydrogen will react with an equal volume of chlorine to produce twice that volume of hydrogen chloride.

100 cm³ of hydrogen will react with 100 cm³ to produce 200 cm³ of hydrogen chloride.

daydream
EDUCATION

Reactivity of Metals

The Reactivity Series

The reactivity series lists metals in order of their reactivity.

The ease by which metals lose electrons determines their level of reactivity.

Metals higher up the reactivity series have a greater tendency to lose electrons and form positive ions. Therefore, they are more reactive.

Carbon and hydrogen are not metals, but they are often included in the reactivity series to show how metals in the series can be extracted from their ores. This is explained in more detail in the **Metal Extraction** section.

Potassium	K
Sodium	Na
Lithium	Li
Calcium	Ca
Magnesium	Mg
Carbon	C
Zinc	Zn
Iron	Fe
Hydrogen	H
Copper	Cu

Non-metals

Increased reactivity

Oxidation and Reduction

Reactions of metals often involve the processes of oxidation and reduction.

Oxidation is the addition of oxygen or the removal of electrons.

Reduction is the removal of oxygen or the addition of electrons.

Displacement Reactions

A more reactive metal can displace a less reactive metal from a compound.

Example: If iron is placed in a copper sulfate solution, the iron will displace the copper to form iron sulfate.

$$\text{iron} \quad + \quad \text{copper sulfate} \quad \longrightarrow \quad \text{iron sulfate} \quad + \quad \text{copper}$$
$$\text{Fe} \qquad\qquad \text{CuSO}_4 \qquad\qquad\qquad \text{FeSO}_4 \qquad\qquad \text{Cu}$$

This is an example of a redox reaction in which one substance is reduced and another is oxidised.

In this reaction, the iron atoms are oxidised to form iron ions, and the copper ions are reduced to form copper atoms. The iron atoms lose two electrons (oxidation), whereas the copper ions gain two electrons (reduction).

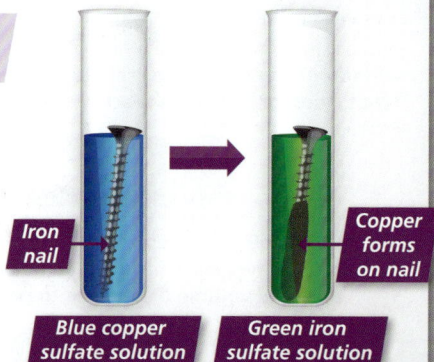

$$Fe \longrightarrow Fe^{2+} + 2e^-$$

$$Cu^{2+} + 2e^- \longrightarrow Cu$$

Iron nail

Copper forms on nail

Blue copper sulfate solution

Green iron sulfate solution

daydream EDUCATION

Reactions with Acids and Water

The higher a metal is in the reactivity series, the more easily it will r...
In all reactions, the metal atoms lose electrons to fo...

metal + acid = salt + hydrogen

metal + water

The...

Reaction with Dilute Acids

	Element	Symbol	
React vigorously to form a salt solution and hydrogen	Potassium	K	...al hydroxide and hydrogen
	Sodium	Na	
	Lithium	Li	
React more slowly to form a salt solution and hydrogen	Calcium	Ca	**React slowly or not at all with cold water; form hydrogen and a metal oxide with steam**
	Magnesium	Mg	
	Zinc	Zn	
	Iron	Fe	
No reaction	Copper	Cu	**No reaction**

Metal Extraction

Carbon and hydrogen are often included in the reactivity series to show how metals can be extracted from their ores. For example, metals such as zinc can be displaced by adding carbon, whereas copper can be displaced by adding carbon or hydrogen.

Metals that are more reactive than carbon, such as aluminium, have to be extracted from their ores using a process called electrolysis. Unreactive metals such as gold and platinum are found as pure elements and do not need to be extracted.

Many metals react with oxygen to form metal oxides (ores) in a process called oxidation. Therefore, to extract a metal from its ore, oxygen needs to be removed in a process called reduction.

The Blast Furnace

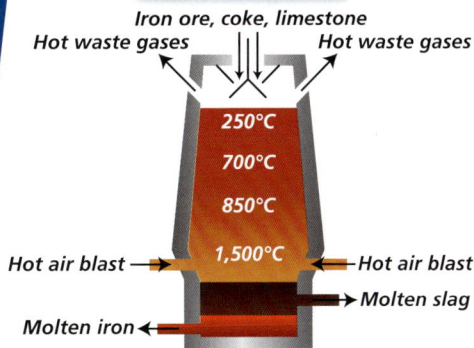

Iron ore, coke, limestone

Hot waste gases — Hot waste gases

250°C

700°C

850°C

1,500°C

Hot air blast → ← Hot air blast

→ Molten slag

Molten iron ←

Iron is extracted from iron oxide by heating it with carbon in a blast furnace. Because carbon is more reactive than iron, it displaces the iron from the iron oxide.

$$\text{iron oxide} \quad + \quad \text{carbon} \quad \longrightarrow \quad \text{iron} \quad + \quad \text{carbon dioxide}$$
$$2Fe_2O_3 \quad + \quad 3C \quad \longrightarrow \quad 4Fe \quad + \quad 3CO_2$$

Iron oxide is reduced (loses oxygen) to form iron.
Carbon is oxidised (gains oxygen) to form carbon dioxide.

and Alkalis

The pH Scale

pH scale is a measure of the acidity or alkalinity of a solution. It can be measured by a universal indicator, which changes colour depending on the pH of the solution. The colours for each pH are shown below. A digital pH probe and meter can also be used to measure the pH of a solution.

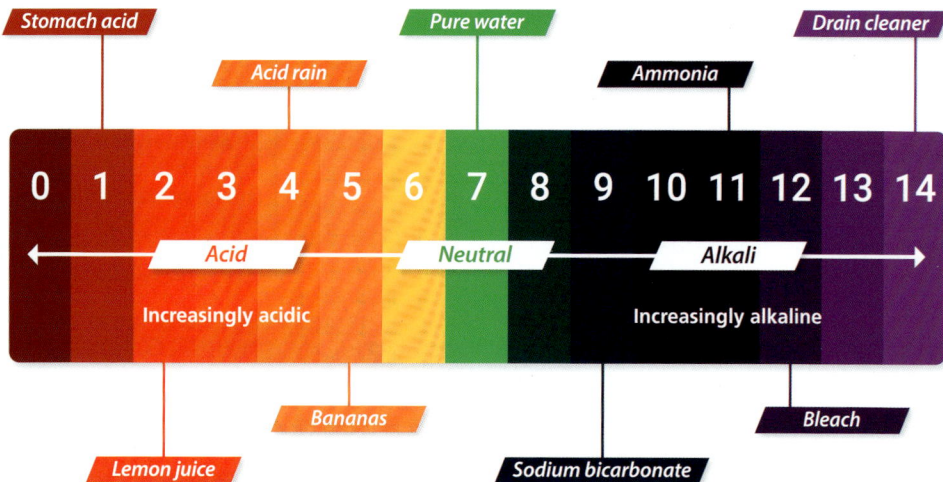

Stomach acid

Acid rain

Pure water

Ammonia

Drain cleaner

| 0 | 1 | 2 | 3 | 4 | 5 | 6 | 7 | 8 | 9 | 10 | 11 | 12 | 13 | 14 |

Acid — Neutral — Alkali

Increasingly acidic

Increasingly alkaline

Lemon juice

Bananas

Sodium bicarbonate

Bleach

A base is a substance that neutralises an acid. An alkali is a soluble base. All alkalis are bases, but not all bases are alkalis.

Acids produce an excess of hydrogen ions (H^+) in aqueous solutions (aq).

As the number of hydrogen ions in a certain volume increases, the lower the pH level and the more acidic the solution.

When acids and alkalis react, hydrogen ions react with hydroxide ions to produce water. This is called neutralisation.

$$acid + alkali \rightarrow water$$
$$H^+_{(aq)} \quad OH^-_{(aq)} \quad H_2O_{(l)}$$

Alkalis produce an excess of hydroxide ions (OH^-) in aqueous solutions (aq).

As the number of hydroxide ions in a certain volume increases, the higher the pH level and the more alkaline the solution.

The pH scale is a measure of the concentration of hydrogen ions in a solution. As the pH level increases by one unit, the hydrogen ion concentration of the solution decreases by a factor of 10.

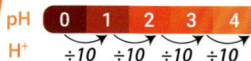

pH	0	1	2	3	4
H^+		$\div 10$	$\div 10$	$\div 10$	$\div 10$

daydream
EDUCATION

Reactions of Acids

Acids react with metals to produce salts and hydrogen. The salt that is produced in any reaction depends on the **acid used** and the positive ions in the metal or base.

acid + metal $\rightarrow$ salt + hydrogen

acid + metal hydroxide $\rightarrow$ salt + water

acid + metal oxide $\rightarrow$ salt + water

Hydrochloric acid produces chlorides:

hydrochloric acid + magnesium $\rightarrow$ magnesium chloride + hydrogen
$2HCl$ + Mg $\rightarrow$ $MgCl_2$ + H_2

Nitric acid produces nitrates:

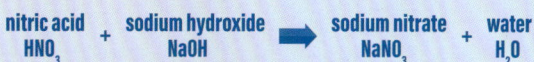

nitric acid + sodium hydroxide $\rightarrow$ sodium nitrate + water
HNO_3 + $NaOH$ $\rightarrow$ $NaNO_3$ + H_2O

Sulfuric acid produces sulfates:

sulfuric acid + copper oxide $\rightarrow$ copper sulfate + water
H_2SO_4 + CuO $\rightarrow$ $CuSO_4$ + H_2O

Metal carbonates neutralise acids to produce salt, water and carbon dioxide.

acid + metal carbonate $\rightarrow$ salt + water + carbon dioxide

sulfuric acid + copper carbonate $\rightarrow$ copper sulfate + water + carbon dioxide
H_2SO_4 + $CuCO_3$ $\rightarrow$ $CuSO_4$ + H_2O + CO_2

You can make a soluble salt by neutralising an acid with a base, such as an insoluble metal oxide, hydroxide or carbonate.

Step 1

Gently heat the acid, add the insoluble base and stir.

Step 2

Keep adding the base until there is no more reaction. This means there is excess base.

Step 3

Filter out the excess base from the solution.

Step 4

Heat the solution to evaporate some of the water. Then leave it to cool to allow salt crystals to form.

The reactions between acids and metals are redox reactions. The metal loses electrons and so is oxidised. The hydrogen gains electrons and so is reduced.

When magnesium reacts with hydrochloric acid, the magnesium is oxidised (loses electrons), forming magnesium chloride, whereas the hydrochloric acid is reduced (gaining electrons), forming hydrogen gas.

$Mg \rightarrow Mg^{2+} + 2e^-$

$2H^+ + 2e^- \rightarrow H_2$

$Mg + 2H^-Cl^- \rightarrow Mg^{2+}Cl^-_2 + H_2$

daydream
EDUCATION

Strong and Weak Acids

All acids ionise (produce protons) in aqueous solution.

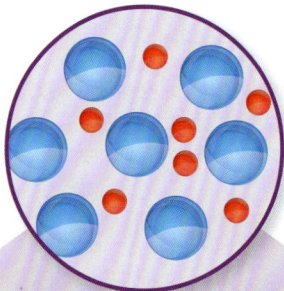

A strong acid is one that is completely ionised in aqueous solution, so it releases a lot of hydrogen (H⁺) ions.

Examples include hydrochloric, sulfuric and nitric acids.

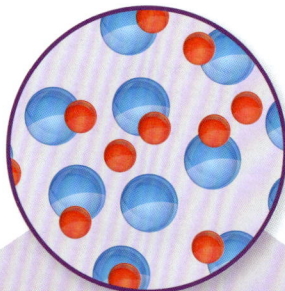

Weak acids are only partially ionised in aqueous solution. They are less reactive.

Examples include ethanoic, citric and carbonic acids.

● Hydrogen ion ● Undissociated molecule

As pH decreases by one unit, the hydrogen ion concentration increases by a factor of 10.

Strong and weak are not the same as concentrated and dilute. A concentrated acid contains a high proportion of acid to water in the aqueous solution, whereas a dilute acid contains a lower proportion. Adding water to a strong acid dilutes it but does not turn it into a weak acid.

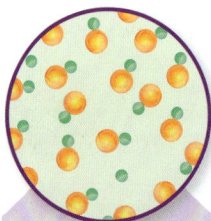

Weak, concentrated ethanoic acid

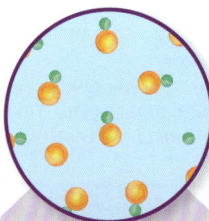

Weak, dilute ethanoic acid

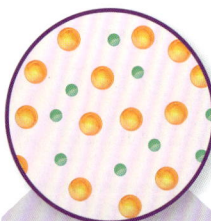

Strong, concentrated hydrochloric acid

Strong, dilute hydrochloric acid

● Acid (CH_3COOH, HCL)   ● Conjugate base (CH_3COO^-(aq), Cl^-(aq))   ● H^+(aq)

daydream
EDUCATION

Titrations

Titrations are used to determine the concentration of acids and alkalis.

To determine the concentration of an alkali of a known volume, an acid of a known concentration and volume is added to the alkaline solution until neutralisation occurs. Conversely, an alkali is used to identify an acid's concentration.

At the exact point of neutralisation (the end point of the reaction), equivalent mole amounts of acid and alkali have reacted with each other, so it is possible to calculate the unknown concentration, measured in moles per decimetre cubed (mol/dm^3).

The number of moles of acid and alkali that react will be indicated in a balanced chemical equation for the reaction.

1 Use a pipette and pipette filler to measure the alkali (of unknown concentration).

2 Add the alkali and a few drops of an indicator to a conical flask.

3 Use a funnel to fill a burette with an acid of known concentration, and record the initial volume.

4 Slowly add the acid to the alkali and mix the solution after each addition.

5 When the indicator changes colour (i.e. neutralisation occurs), record the volume of acid remaining in the burette and calculate the volume that was required to neutralise the alkali.

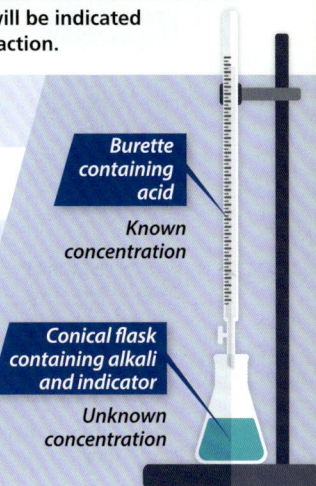

Burette containing acid

Known concentration

Conical flask containing alkali and indicator

Unknown concentration

This information can now be used to calculate the concentration of the alkali.

Example

A student uses a pipette to add 25 cm^3 of sodium hydroxide of unknown concentration to a conical flask, along with a few drops of phenolphthalein indicator.

The student then performs a titration to find that 20 cm^3 of 0.5 mol/dm^3 hydrochloric acid was required to neutralise the sodium hydroxide. The equation for the reaction is:

$$HCl + NaOH \longrightarrow NaCl + H_2O$$

Calculate the concentration of the sodium hydroxide.

The number of moles in 20 cm^3 of 0.5 mol/dm^3 hydrochloric acid is calculated as follows:

Volume = 20 cm^3 = 0.02 dm^3

Moles = concentration × volume = 0.5 × 0.02 = 0.01 mol

The equation for the reaction shows that 1 mol of HCl reacts with 1 mol of NaOH. Therefore, there were 0.01 moles of NaOH in the 25 cm^3 solution, as 0.01 mol of HCl reacted with 0.01 mol of NaOH.

The concentration of sodium hydroxide can now be calculated:

$$\text{Concentration} = \frac{\text{moles}}{\text{volume}} = \frac{0.01}{0.025} = 0.4 \ mol/dm^3$$

Electrolysis

Electrolysis is the process by which ionic substances are decomposed (broken down) into simpler substances when an electric current is passed through them.

When an ionic compound is dissolved in water or melted to form an electrolyte, its ions are free to move about and conduct electricity. During electrolysis, an electric current is passed through the electrolyte to break it down into simpler substances.

- Electrodes are usually made of carbon (graphite).
- Electrodes are inert. This means they do not form ions during electrolysis.
- Ions are discharged (lose their charge) at the electrodes.

Don't PANIC!
Positive is Anode
Negative is Cathode

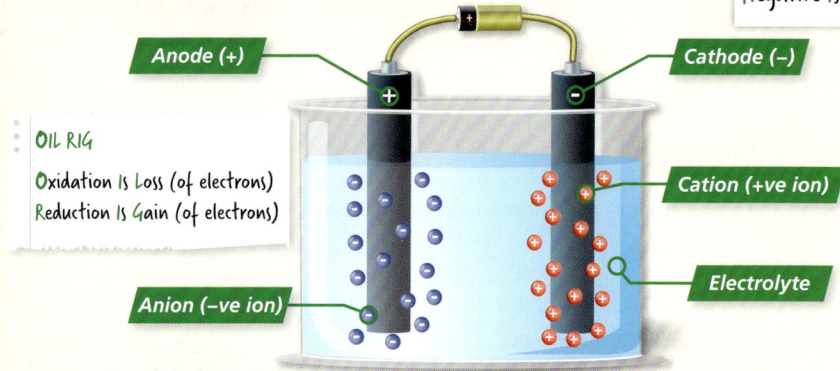

Anode (+)

Cathode (−)

OIL RIG
Oxidation Is Loss (of electrons)
Reduction Is Gain (of electrons)

Cation (+ve ion)

Anion (−ve ion)

Electrolyte

Negative Ions (Anions)

Negative ions (anions) are attracted to the positively charged anode, where they lose electrons to form atoms.

This is oxidation. It can be shown as a half-equation:

$$X^- - e^- \Rightarrow X \text{ or } X^- \Rightarrow X + e^-$$

Positive Ions (Cations)

Positive ions (cations) are attracted to the negatively charged cathode, where they gain electrons to form atoms.

This is reduction. It can be shown as a half-equation:

$$Y^+ + e^- \Rightarrow Y$$

Electrolysis of Molten Ionic Compounds

When a simple ionic compound is electrolysed in a molten state, the metal is always produced at the cathode and the non-metal is always produced at the anode.

lead (II) bromide $\Rightarrow$ lead + bromine

Bromine molecules (Br_2) formed at the anode:

$$2Br^- \Rightarrow Br_2 + 2e^-$$

Lead (Pb) atoms formed at the cathode:

$$Pb^{2+} + 2e^- \Rightarrow Pb$$

Molten lead (II) bromide

Negative bromide ions attracted to the positive electrode

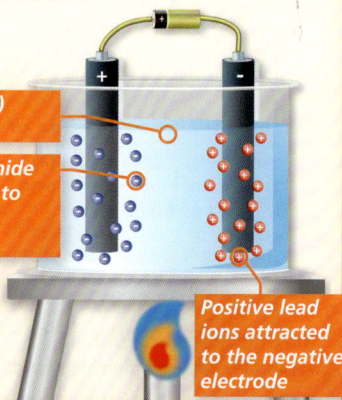

Positive lead ions attracted to the negative electrode

Compound	Product at Cathode	Product at Anode
Sodium chloride (NaCl)	Sodium (Na)	Chlorine (Cl_2)
Magnesium oxide (MgO)	Magnesium (Mg)	Oxygen (O_2)

daydream
EDUCATION

Electrolysis to Extract Metals

Metals above carbon in the reactivity series must be extracted by electrolysis. Electrolysis requires lots of energy to melt the compounds and to produce the electrical current, so it is very expensive.

It is used to extract aluminium from bauxite (aluminium oxide). **aluminium oxide ➡ aluminium + oxygen**

As bauxite has a very high melting point, it is dissolved in molten cryolite (another oxide of aluminium), which has a lower melting point.

Positive electrodes (anodes)

The negative oxide ions are attracted to the anodes, where they lose electrons to form oxygen.

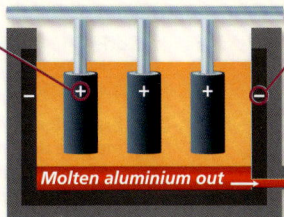

$$2O^{2-} \implies O_2 + 4e^-$$

Molten aluminium out

Negative electrode (cathode)

The positive aluminium ions are attracted to the cathode, where they gain electrons to form aluminium.

$$Al^{3+} + 3e^- \implies Al$$

At the anode, the oxygen formed reacts with the carbon electrodes to form carbon dioxide. This means that the anodes frequently have to be replaced.

$$C(s) + O_2(g) \implies CO_2(g)$$

Electrolysis of Aqueous Solutions

When an aqueous solution is electrolysed, the ions discharged depend on the reactivity of the elements involved. Hydrogen is produced at the cathode if the metal is more reactive than hydrogen. At the positive electrode, oxygen is produced unless the solution contains halide ions when the halogen is produced.

Copper Chloride Solution

When copper chloride dissolves in water, a mixture of ions is present.

The copper chloride breaks down into copper ions (Cu^{2+}) and chloride ions (Cl^-).

$$CuCl_2 \implies Cu^{2+} + 2Cl^-$$

The water molecules break down, producing hydrogen ions (H^+) and hydroxide ions (OH^-).

$$H_2O \implies H^+ + OH^-$$

Chloride ions are discharged to form chlorine gas

Copper ions are discharged to form copper atoms

Copper chloride solution

Negative ions are attracted to the anode

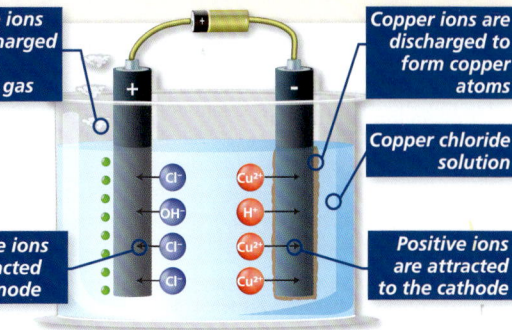

Positive ions are attracted to the cathode

$$2Cl^- \implies Cl_2 + 2e^- \qquad Cu^{2+} + 2e^- \implies Cu$$

Aqueous Solution	Ions Present	At the Cathode	At the Anode
Sodium chloride (NaCl)	Na^+, Cl^-, H^+, OH^-	Sodium is more reactive than hydrogen, so hydrogen ions are discharged to form hydrogen: $2H^+ + 2e^- \implies H_2$	Chloride ions are discharged to form chlorine: $2Cl^- \implies Cl_2 + 2e^-$
Copper sulfate ($CuSO_4$)	Cu^{2+}, SO_4^{2-}, H^+, OH^-	Copper is less reactive than hydrogen, so copper ions are discharged to form copper: $Cu^{2+} + 2e^- \implies Cu$	No halide ions are present, so hydroxide ions are discharged to form water and oxygen: $4OH^- \implies O_2 + 2H_2O + 4e^-$

Exothermic & Endothermic Reactions

In chemical reactions, energy is conserved. This means that the amount of energy is the same at the end of a chemical reaction as it was before the reaction took place.

Exothermic Reactions

In an exothermic reaction, heat energy is given out, and the temperature of the surroundings increases.

The reactants have more energy than the products, so energy is given out.

Examples of exothermic reactions include combustion (burning), many oxidation reactions and neutralisation. Exothermic reactions are used in self-heating cans and hand warmers.

During exothermic reactions, the energy released through the formation of bonds is greater than the energy used to break bonds.

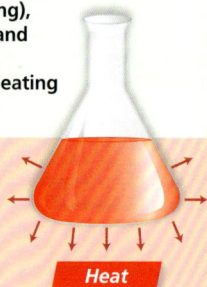

Heat

Endothermic Reactions

In an endothermic reaction, heat energy is taken in, and the temperature of the surroundings decreases.

The reactants have less energy than the products, so energy is taken in.

Examples of endothermic reactions include thermal decomposition and the reaction of citric acid and sodium hydrogen carbonate. Endothermic reactions are used in some sports injury cold packs.

During endothermic reactions, the energy used to break bonds is greater than the energy released through the formation of bonds.

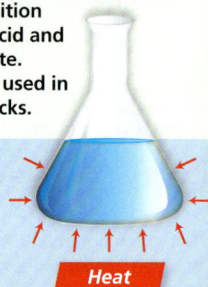

Heat

Reaction Profiles

Chemical reactions occur only when particles collide with each other with sufficient energy. The minimum amount of energy that particles must have to react is called the activation energy.

Reaction profiles are used to show the relative energies of the reactants and products in a reaction and how energy changes during the reaction.

Energetic collision leads to product

No reaction

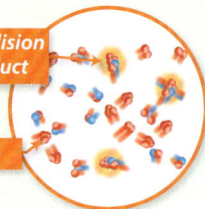

Exothermic Reaction Profile

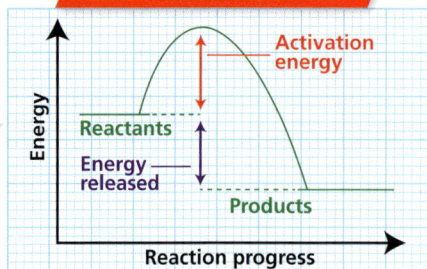

Energy

Activation energy

Reactants

Energy released

Products

Reaction progress

The products are at a lower energy level than the reactants.

Endothermic Reaction Profile

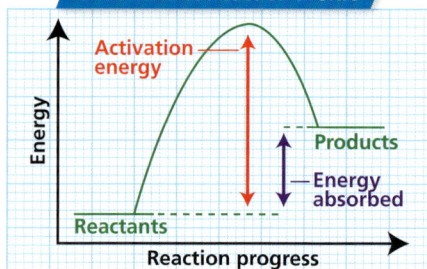

Energy

Activation energy

Products

Energy absorbed

Reactants

Reaction progress

The products are at a higher energy level than the reactants.

daydream EDUCATION

Measuring Energy Transfer

You can measure the amount of energy released in a chemical reaction (in solution) by measuring the temperature change during the reaction.

method

1. Add one reactant to the cup and measure the temperature.
2. Add the other reactant and mix.
3. Measure the temperature of the solution at the end of the reaction.
4. If the temperature increases, the reaction is exothermic. If it decreases, the reaction is endothermic.

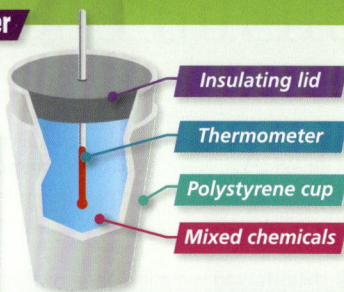

Insulating lid

Thermometer

Polystyrene cup

Mixed chemicals

The insulating lid and polystyrene cup help limit the amount of energy lost to the surroundings.

Bond Energies

When a chemical bond is formed, energy is released, making it an exothermic reaction. To break a bond, energy needs to be supplied, making it an endothermic reaction. Bond energies are different for different bonds.

The energy required to make a bond in a substance is the same as the energy required to break the same bond.

$+ 242 \text{ kJ/mol}$

$- 242 \text{ kJ/mol}$

Cl_2 Cl Cl

Examples of Bond Energies

Bond	Bond Energy (kJ/mol)
H-H	436
C-H	413
C=O	743
O=O	496
H-Cl	432
Cl-Cl	242

Calculating Energy Change in a Reaction

You can use the different bond energies in a reaction to calculate the overall energy change. The difference between the sum of energy required to break bonds in the reactants and the sum of the energy released when bonds in the products are made is the overall energy change.

What is the overall energy change in the reaction of methane with oxygen to produce carbon dioxide and water?

Chemical equation

$$CH_4 + 2O_2 \longrightarrow CO_2 + 2H_2O$$

1	Identify the bond energies for each compound or molecule.	C-H = 413 kJ/mol C=O = 743 kJ/mol O=O = 496 kJ/mol O-H = 463 kJ/mol
2	Identify the number of bonds in the equation.	$4 \times$ C-H $2 \times$ O=O $2 \times$ C=O $4 \times$ O-H
3	Calculate the bond energies for the reactants and the products.	$4 \times 413 + 2 \times 496$ $2 \times 743 + 4 \times 463$ 2,644 kJ/mol 3,338 kJ/mol
4	Calculate the energy change in the reaction.	energy to break bonds – energy to form bonds $2,644 - 3,338 = -694$ kJ/mol

The overall energy change is −694 kJ/mol.
As more energy is released than is used, the reaction is exothermic.

Chemical Cells & Fuel Cells

Cells contain chemicals that react to produce electricity. A battery consists of two or more **chemical cells** in series.

Chemical Cells

A chemical cell is made by connecting two electrodes with a wire and placing them in an electrolyte, or salt solution.

- Each electrode must be of a material that conducts electricity (usually metal) and must have different reactivities.

- The electrolyte must be a solution of an ionic compound so that it will provide ions to carry the current from one electrode to the other.

A Chemical Cell

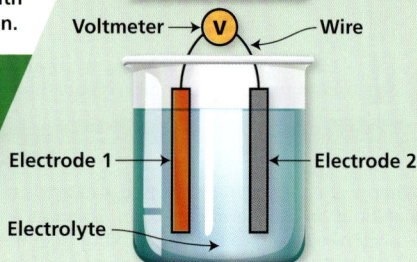

Voltmeter — V — Wire

Electrode 1 — — Electrode 2

Electrolyte

Because of different reactivities, there is a **potential difference** (voltage) between the two metals that causes electrons to flow through the wires, creating a current. The flow of ions in the electrolyte completes the circuit.

Cell Voltage

The voltage produced by chemical cells depends on multiple factors, including the electrodes and electrolyte used.

The greater the difference in reactivity between the two metals, the higher the voltage. The electrolyte used and its concentration can affect the voltage too as different ions will react differently with the metal electrodes used.

Rechargeable and Non-Rechargeable Cells

In some cells, the reactions that occur at the electrodes are non-reversible. Once one of the reactants has been used up, a cell can no longer produce a voltage. Such cells are non-rechargeable, the type used in alkaline batteries.

However, if the electrode materials and the electrolyte react reversibly, the cells can be recharged by passing a current through them.

Fuel Cells

Unlike in non-rechargeable batteries, which are sealed, the reactants in fuel cells can be replaced once they have been used up. This means that they can be run continuously, making them a potential alternative to rechargeable cells and batteries.

daydream EDUCATION

How Fuel Cells Work

A fuel cell is supplied with an external source of fuel, usually hydrogen, and oxygen. The fuel is then electrochemically oxidised, creating a potential difference.

In a fuel cell, the electrolyte varies, but potassium hydroxide, sodium hydroxide and phosphoric acid are common electrolytes.

Unlike in electrolysis, the cathode in a fuel cell is positive, and the anode is negative. Also, the positive and negative symbols indicate electron gain and loss, not charge. Reduction occurs at the cathode, and oxidation occurs at the anode.

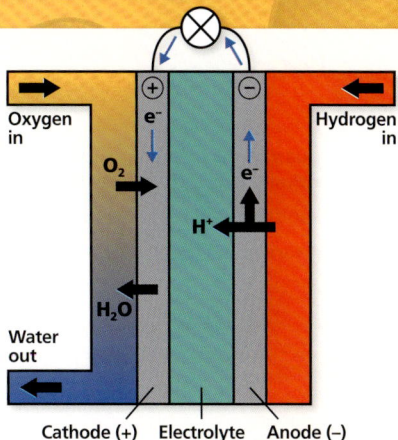

Oxygen in

O_2

H_2O

Water out

Hydrogen in

e^-

e^-

H^+

Cathode (+)   Electrolyte   Anode (–)

Through oxidation at the anode, hydrogen loses electrons to form hydrogen ions.

$$2H_2 \longrightarrow 4H^+ + 4e^-$$

The hydrogen ions move through the electrolyte to the other electrode.
The newly formed electrons move through a wire to the cathode, creating a current.
Through reduction at the cathode, the hydrogen ions and electrons react with oxygen to form water.

$$O_2 + 4H^+ + 4e^- \longrightarrow 2H_2O$$

Advantages and Disadvantages of Fuel Cells

+ Hydrogen fuel cells used in vehicles produce no pollution, only water.

+ Compared to batteries, fuel cells last longer and contain fewer toxic (metal) compounds that can harm the environment upon disposal.

+ Fuel cells can run continuously. In contrast, non-rechargeable batteries have a limited life, and rechargeable batteries cannot be used while recharging.

– Hydrogen is an explosive gas. Storing it is dangerous and requires a lot of space.

– Fuel cells are much more expensive than batteries.

– Producing hydrogen, either from methane or by using electricity to electrolyse water, involves the use of fossil fuels and the release of greenhouse gases.

daydream
EDUCATION

Rate of Reaction

Chemical reactions can occur at vastly different rates. The reactivity of the reactants is a major factor in determining the rate, but other variables also have an effect.

Calculating Rates of Reaction

The rate of a chemical reaction can be measured by measuring either the quantity of reactant used or the quantity of product formed over a given time.

$$\text{mean rate of reaction} = \frac{\text{quantity of reactant used}}{\text{time taken}}$$

$$\text{mean rate of reaction} = \frac{\text{quantity of product formed}}{\text{time taken}}$$

The quantity of reactant used or product formed is usually measured in mass (g) or by volume (cm^3). Therefore, the unit for the rate of reaction is either g/s or cm^3/s.

Quantities are also measured in moles, with the rate of reaction unit being mol/s.

The measurements are means because the reaction rate often varies during the time taken.

The rate of a reaction can be measured in various ways, including:

| Volume of gas collected per unit time | Time taken for a colour change or a change in turbidity | Increase in temperature per unit time in the reaction mixture (for exothermic reactions) | Decrease in mass of a reactant or increase in mass of a product per unit time |

Rates of Reaction Graphs

Graphs can be created to show the quantity of a reactant consumed or the quantity of a product formed against time. The example below shows the quantity of a product formed against time.

The steeper the line of the graph, the faster the rate of reaction. Over time, the line will generally get shallower as more of the reactants are consumed.

The reaction represented by the blue line produces the most amount of product. It starts off relatively quickly and finishes the latest.

The reaction represented by the green line produces the second most amount of product. It starts off the fastest and ends the quickest.

The reaction represented by the orange line produces the least amount of product. It starts off the slowest and finishes relatively quickly.

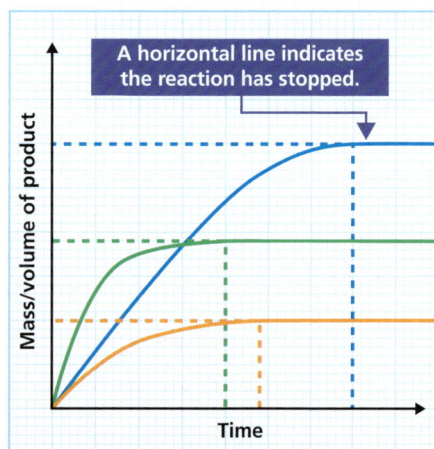

A horizontal line indicates the reaction has stopped.

Mass/volume of product

Time

daydream
EDUCATION

Calculating Rates of Reaction Using Graphs

The rate of reaction between two times can be calculated using a graph. Simply divide the change in values on the y-axis by the change in values on the x-axis.

The graph below shows the volume of gas produced in an experiment over a period of time. Calculate the mean rate of reaction between 10 and 30 seconds.

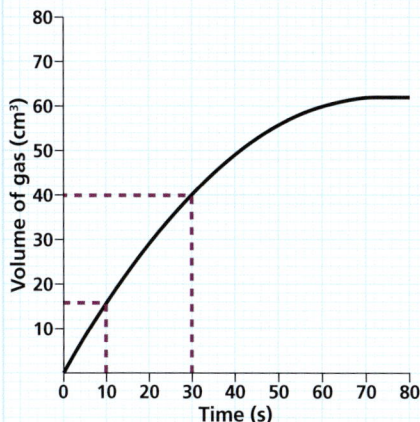

1 Find 10 seconds and 30 seconds on the x-axis, and draw lines up to the rate of reaction line.

2 From the points where these lines touch the rate of reaction line, draw horizontal lines to the y-axis.

3 Calculate the rate of reaction.

$$\text{mean rate of reaction} = \frac{\text{change in } y}{\text{change in } x}$$

$$= \frac{40 - 16}{30 - 10}$$

$$= \frac{24}{20}$$

$$= 1.2 \text{ cm}^3/\text{s}$$

The rate of reaction at a specific time can also be measured by calculating the gradient of a tangent to the curve on the graph.

The graph below shows the volume of gas produced in an experiment over a period of time. Calculate the rate of reaction at 30 seconds.

1 Find the point on the line that aligns vertically with 30 seconds on the x-axis.

2 Place your ruler on the line, and draw a tangent to this point (30 seconds). (Ensure the tangent extends across the graph.)

3 Pick two points on the tangent and calculate its gradient.

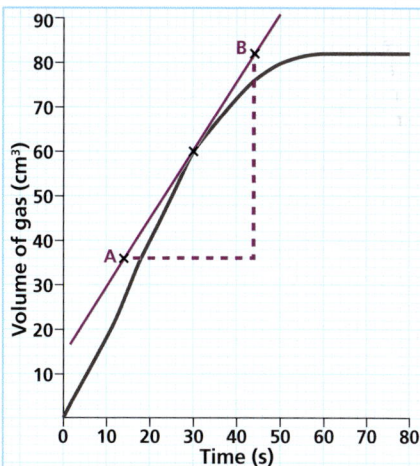

$$\text{gradient} = \frac{\text{change in } y}{\text{change in } x}$$

$$= \frac{82 - 36}{44 - 14}$$

$$= \frac{46}{30}$$

$$= 1.53 \text{ cm}^3/\text{s (2 d.p.)}$$

The rate of reaction at 30 seconds was 1.53 cm³/s.

Collision Theory

Collision theory states that chemical reactions happen when reactant particles collide, as long as there is sufficient energy to start a reaction. The minimum amount of energy needed to start a given reaction is called the activation energy.

A certain proportion of collisions will be 'successful collisions' – that is, they will have enough energy to cause a reaction.

There are various factors that can increase the frequency of collisions, the number of successful collisions and the reaction rate.

Energetic collision leads to product

No reaction

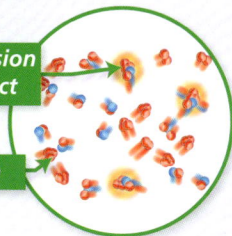

Factors Affecting the Rates of Chemical Reactions

The following factors affect the rate of chemical reactions:

Temperature	An increase in temperature increases the rate of reaction as the particles have more energy, move around quicker and collide more frequently.
Concentration of the Reactant	An increase in the concentration of the reactants in a solution increases the rate of reaction because there are more particles in a given volume. This means that the particles will collide more frequently.
Pressure of Reacting Gases	An increase in the pressure of reacting gases also means that there are more particles within a given volume and the particles will collide more frequently.
Surface Area of a Solid Reactant	Increasing the surface area of a solid (e.g. by making it into a powder) increases the rate of reaction because more particles are exposed to the other reactants, resulting in more collisions.
Presence of a Catalyst	A catalyst is a substance that increases the rate of a chemical reaction without itself undergoing any permanent chemical change. Catalysts work by providing a different pathway with a lower activation energy for the reaction. Because catalysts are not reactants, they are not included in the chemical equation for the reaction.

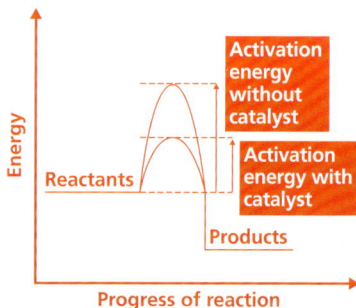

Activation energy without catalyst

Activation energy with catalyst

Reactants

Products

Energy

Progress of reaction

A decrease in these factors or the absence of a catalyst decreases the rate of reaction.

daydream EDUCATION

Reversible Reactions

In some reactions, the products react with each other to reform the reactants. These are reversible reactions.

The equation for a reversible reaction has a double arrow to show that the reaction can go in either direction.

Products	forwards	Reactants
A + B		C + D
	backwards	

The overall direction of reversible reactions can be changed by changing the conditions.

ammonium chloride   heat / cool   ammonia + hydrogen chloride

Ammonium chloride is broken down into ammonia and hydrogen chloride when it is heated.

Ammonia can react with hydrogen chlorine to reform ammonium chloride when cooled.

Energy Changes

If a reversible reaction is exothermic in one direction, it will be endothermic in the other. The same amount of energy will be transferred in each case.

In this reaction, there is an energy change of +78 kJ when the hydrated copper sulfate is heated to form anhydrous copper sulfate and water in an **endothermic reaction**.

endothermic

hydrated copper sulfate   anhydrous copper sulfate + water

exothermic

Conversely, there is an energy change of −78 kJ when the anhydrous copper sulfate is rehydrated with water in an **exothermic** reaction.

Equilibrium

In a closed system (from which reactants or products cannot escape), a reversible reaction will eventually reach equilibrium, where the forward and backward reactions are occurring at the same rate.

Reaching equilibrium does not mean that there is an equal amount (concentration) of products and reactants. Rather, it means that the amount of the respective reactants and products is constant.

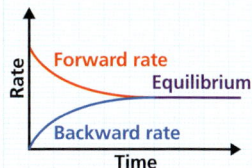

Equilibrium Position Left

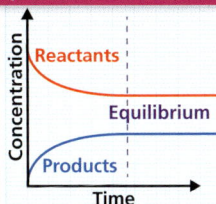

There are more reactants than products at equilibrium.

Equilibrium Position Centre

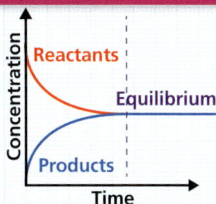

The amount of reactants and the products is the same.

Equilibrium Position Right

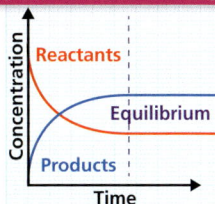

There are more products than reactants at equilibrium.

Factors Affecting Reversible Reactions

Le Chatelier's Principle

The relative amounts of reactants and products at equilibrium depend on the conditions of the reaction. Le Chatelier's principle states that if a system is at equilibrium and a change is made to its conditions, the system will respond to counteract the change.

Change in Temperature

In the case of an exothermic or endothermic reaction:

If there is a decrease in temperature, the equilibrium will shift in the exothermic direction to counteract this and raise the temperature.

If the forward reaction is exothermic and the backward reaction is endothermic, the equilibrium position shifts to the right, increasing the concentration of products and decreasing the concentration of reactants.

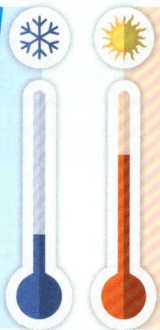

If there is an increase in temperature, the equilibrium will shift in the endothermic direction to counteract this and lower the temperature.

If the forward reaction is exothermic and the backward reaction is endothermic, the equilibrium position shifts to the left, decreasing the concentration of products and increasing the concentration of reactants.

Change in Concentration

When the concentration of a reactant or a product changes, the concentration of the substance will change until equilibrium is re-established.

Increase in Concentration

If there is an increase in reactant concentration, the equilibrium will shift towards the products to re-establish equilibrium. This will decrease the concentration of reactants and increase the concentration of products.

Decrease in Concentration

If there is a decrease in reactant concentration, the equilibrium will shift towards the reactants to re-establish equilibrium. This will increase the concentration of reactants and decrease the concentration of products.

Change in Pressure

Changing the pressure in a reverse reaction only affects gases.

An increase in pressure shifts the equilibrium towards the side with fewer molecules.

A decrease in pressure shifts the equilibrium towards the side with more molecules.

daydream
EDUCATION

Crude Oil

Crude oil is a finite resource found in rocks. It is used as a raw material in many products, including solvents, fuels, detergents and plastics.

How Crude Oil Forms

Crude oil is a fossil fuel that has formed over millions of years from the remains of biomass (mainly plankton) that was buried in mud.

Organisms die and fall to the sea bed.

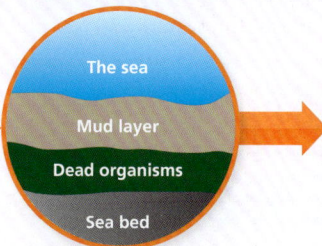

They get covered in layers of mud.

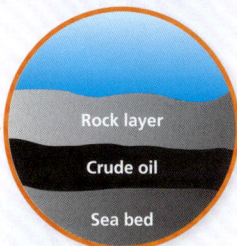

The mud turns into rock, and the organisms decay to form crude oil.

Crude oil is a mixture of many different compounds, most of which are hydrocarbons (molecules made of only hydrogen and carbon atoms).

Hydrocarbons exist as chains of different lengths and rings; all have a carbon atom backbone.

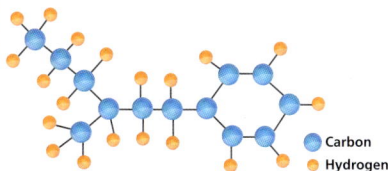

Carbon
Hydrogen

Alkanes

Most of the hydrocarbons in crude oil belong to the alkanes, a series of hydrocarbons that share the same general formula:

$$C_nH_{2n+2}$$

Methane (CH_4)

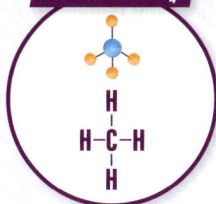

H
|
H—C—H
|
H

Ethane (C_2H_6)

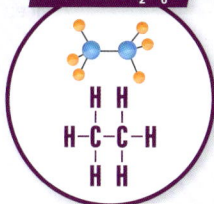

H H
| |
H—C—C—H
| |
H H

Propane (C_3H_8)

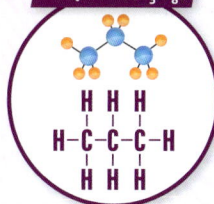

H H H
| | |
H—C—C—C—H
| | |
H H H

Butane (C_4H_{10})

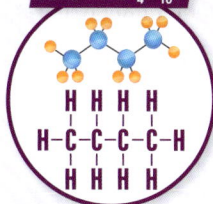

H H H H
| | | |
H—C—C—C—C—H
| | | |
H H H H

Formula

If you know the number of carbon or hydrogen atoms in an alkane, you can work out its formula.

The formula of an alkane with 10 carbon atoms is:

$$C_nH_{2n+2}$$
$$C_{10}H_{(2\times10)+2}$$
$$C_{10}H_{22}$$

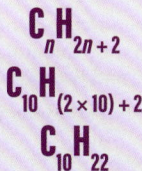

Fractional Distillation

The molecules in crude oil have different lengths and, therefore, different boiling points. This means that they can be separated into mixtures with similar boiling points using fractional distillation.

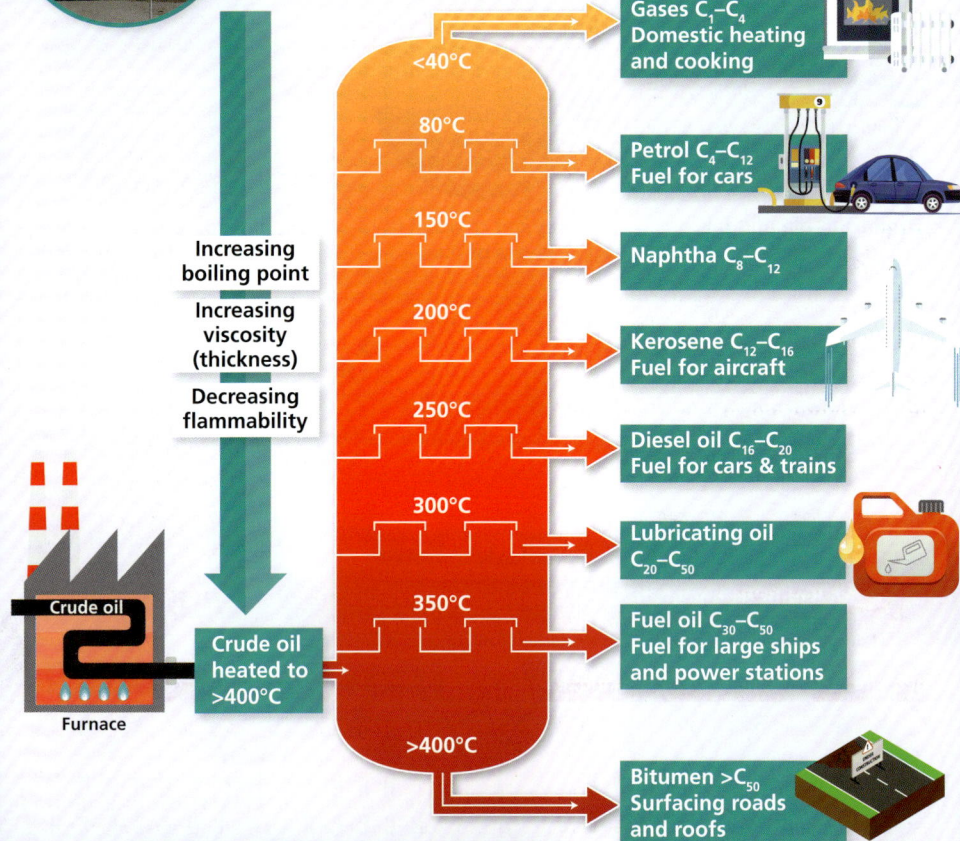

<40°C

Gases C_1–C_4
Domestic heating and cooking

80°C

Petrol C_4–C_{12}
Fuel for cars

150°C

Naphtha C_8–C_{12}

Increasing boiling point

200°C

Kerosene C_{12}–C_{16}
Fuel for aircraft

Increasing viscosity (thickness)

250°C

Diesel oil C_{16}–C_{20}
Fuel for cars & trains

Decreasing flammability

300°C

Lubricating oil C_{20}–C_{50}

350°C

Crude oil

Crude oil heated to >400°C

Fuel oil C_{30}–C_{50}
Fuel for large ships and power stations

Furnace

>400°C

Bitumen >C_{50}
Surfacing roads and roofs

Note: Temperatures and the number of carbons in hydrocarbons are approximates.

The fractionating column is cooler at the top and hotter at the bottom. Crude oil is heated so most of the molecules evaporate and turn into a gas. The gases travel up the column and progressively cool down, causing them to condense at different levels.

The resulting fractions can then be processed into fuels that are vital for modern life. The uses of the different fractions are shown on the diagram above.

daydream EDUCATION

Properties of Hydrocarbons

The ability of carbon atoms to bond together to form families of similar compounds means that there is a vast array of carbon compounds. Many of these are hydrocarbons, which contain only carbon and hydrogen. The properties of hydrocarbons are often related to the size of their molecules.

Boiling Point

As the molecules get larger, they become less volatile and their boiling point gets higher.

Flammability

Fuels need to vaporise to burn. The larger the hydrocarbon molecule, the more difficult it is to vaporise and so the less flammable it is.

Viscosity

Larger chains of molecules have more intermolecular forces and so are more viscous (i.e. less runny).

The properties of hydrocarbons influence how they are used.

Many hydrocarbons are used as fuels. The ones with smaller molecules make the best fuels because they are the most flammable. During combustion, the carbon and hydrogen in the fuel are oxidised (to produce carbon dioxide and water), and energy is released.

Combustion of methane methane CH_4 + oxygen $2O_2$ → carbon dioxide CO_2 + water $2H_2O$

Cracking

Short-chain hydrocarbons are flammable and useful as fuels. Therefore, long-chain hydrocarbons are often broken down into smaller molecules in a process called cracking. Cracking produces short alkanes plus alkenes. Alkenes contain double bonds and can be used to make polymers (plastics).

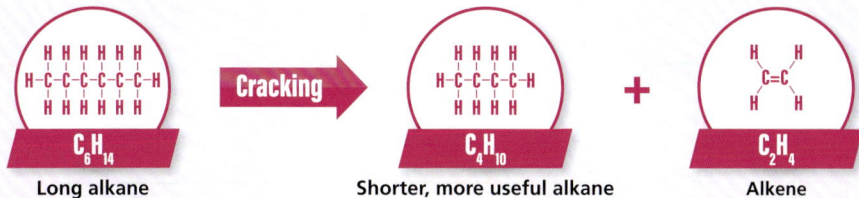

C_6H_{14} — **Cracking** → C_4H_{10} + C_2H_4

Long alkane   Shorter, more useful alkane   Alkene

There are different methods of cracking, each of which produces a mix of different types of product.

- **Catalytic cracking** involves heating long-chain alkenes to vaporise them and then passing them over a catalyst (often silica-alumina) to speed up their breakdown.

- **Steam cracking** involves heating long-chain alkenes to vaporise them and mixing them with steam. The mixture is then heated to around 850°C for a few milliseconds in the absence of oxygen to breakdown the long-chain hydrocarbons into short alkanes and alkenes.

Testing for Alkenes

Alkenes can be distinguished from alkanes by their reaction with orange bromine water.

Alkanes do not react with bromine water, but alkenes are more reactive and remove the bromine, so the bromine water turns colourless.

Alkane   Alkene

Alkenes

Alkenes are a group of **hydrocarbons** that have a double carbon-carbon bond in their molecule. They form a **homologous series** with a general formula of C_nH_{2n}.

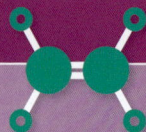

A homologous series is a group of chemicals which have similar chemical properties and can be represented by a general formula.

The first four alkenes and their formulae are shown below:

Name	Molecular Formula	Structural Formula
Ethene	C_2H_4	
Propene	C_3H_6	
Butene	C_4H_8	
Pentene	C_5H_{10}	

Note: Butene and pentene exist in different forms because the position of the C=C bond can vary.

Alkenes are called unsaturated hydrocarbons because they are not 'saturated' with hydrogen. The C=C bond means that alkenes have two fewer hydrogen atoms than alkanes with the same number of carbon atoms.

It is possible to attach extra hydrogen atoms if the double bond is broken.

Reactions of Alkenes

Alkenes are hydrocarbons with the functional group C=C. They burn in oxygen to form carbon dioxide and water.

$$C_2H_4 \ + \ 3O_2 \ \longrightarrow \ 2CO_2 \ + \ 2H_2O$$

If there is insufficient oxygen available, **incomplete combustion** occurs, forming carbon (soot/smoke) and carbon monoxide. Alkenes tend to burn in the air with smoky flames.

Alkenes have a higher proportion of carbon than alkanes, making incomplete combustion more likely.

daydream EDUCATION

The addition of atoms across the C=C bond causes alkenes to react with hydrogen, water and halogens, turning the double bond into a single bond (C-C).

Reaction with Halogens

Alkenes react with halogens, including bromine, fluorine and iodine.

When an alkene is added to bromine water, the carbon-carbon double bond breaks and a **bromine atom** attaches to each carbon atom.

This is an addition reaction as the bromine atoms have combined with the alkene molecules to form a larger molecule.

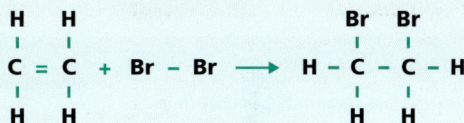

Alkenes decolourise orange bromine water, so bromine water is used as a test for alkenes.

$$\begin{array}{ccc} H \quad H & & Br \quad Br \\ | \quad | & & | \quad | \\ C = C + Br - Br \longrightarrow H - C - C - H \\ | \quad | & & | \quad | \\ H \quad H & & H \quad H \end{array}$$

| Ethene | Bromine | 1,2-Dibromoethane |

Reaction with Hydrogen

The addition of hydrogen – at 150°C with a nickel catalyst – converts alkenes into alkanes.

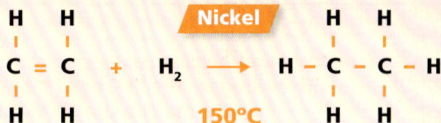

A reaction caused by the addition of hydrogen is known as **hydrogenation**.

$$\begin{array}{ccc} H \quad H & Nickel & H \quad H \\ | \quad | & & | \quad | \\ C = C + H_2 \longrightarrow H - C - C - H \\ | \quad | & 150°C & | \quad | \\ H \quad H & & H \quad H \end{array}$$

| Ethene | Hydrogen | Ethane |

Reaction with Steam

When alkenes react with steam, water is added across the double bond to form an alcohol.

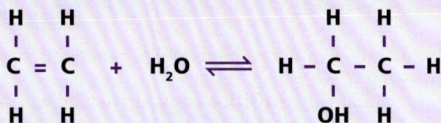

This reaction requires a catalyst and is reversible.

$$\begin{array}{ccc} H \quad H & & H \quad H \\ | \quad | & & | \quad | \\ C = C + H_2O \rightleftharpoons H - C - C - H \\ | \quad | & & | \quad | \\ H \quad H & & OH \quad H \end{array}$$

| Ethene | Water | Ethanol |

Alcohols

Alcohols are a homologous series of organic compounds of the **functional group** –OH. The general formula for alcohols is $C_nH_{2n+1}OH$.

A functional group is an atom or group of atoms joined in a specific way that determines the chemical properties of an organic compound. The first four alcohols in the homologous series are:

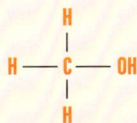
Methanol

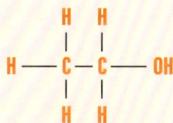
Ethanol

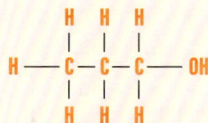
Propanol

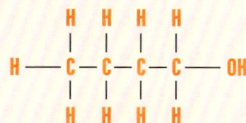
Butanol

Combustion

Alcohols are flammable and burn in oxygen to form carbon dioxide and water. This property of alcohols enables ethanol to be used as a fuel for vehicles.

$$C_2H_5OH + 3O_2 \rightarrow 2CO_2 + 3H_2O$$

Ethanol + Oxygen → Carbon dioxide + Water

Oxidation

Complete oxidation occurs when alcohols are burned in excess oxygen, but partial oxidation by air or oxidising agents converts alcohols into carboxylic acids. For example, in air, ethanol converts to ethanoic acid (vinegar). Wine vinegar is made by exposing wine that contains ethanol to air.

Reaction with Carboxylic Acids — With the aid of a catalyst, alcohols react with carboxylic acids to produce esters.

Reaction with Sodium — Alcohols react with sodium to produce hydrogen gas.

Alcohols and Water

Small alcohol molecules dissolve in water. However, solubility decreases as the length of alcohol molecules increases, so larger molecules do not dissolve as easily with water.

- Ethanol produced by fermentation is the main constituent of all alcoholic drinks.
- Ethanol can be used as fuel in cars with modified engines. In the UK, most petrol contains 5% ethanol.
- Alcohols are good solvents and dissolve some substances that are insoluble in water. They are widely used in perfumes, medicines and mouthwashes.

Making Ethanol

Industrial alcohol can be made by reacting steam with alkenes, but for most uses, ethanol is made by fermenting sugar. The process uses yeast, which feeds on the sugar and converts it into ethanol. This process takes place only in the absence of oxygen (i.e. anaerobically).

Sugar → Ethanol + Carbon dioxide

The alcohol produced contains impurities, which may have to be removed. However, some impurities are left in alcoholic drinks to give them their taste.

daydream EDUCATION

Carboxylic Acids & Esters

Carboxylic acids and esters are both homologous series of organic compounds.

Carboxylic Acids

Carboxylic acids all contain the functional group –COOH.
The first four carboxylic acids and their formulae are shown below.

Name	Molecular Formula	Structural Formula
Methanoic acid	HCOOH	$$\overset{\displaystyle O}{\overset{\|}{H - C - OH}}$$
Ethanoic acid	CH_3COOH	$$H - \overset{H}{\underset{H}{C}} - \overset{O}{C} - OH$$
Propanoic acid	C_2H_5COOH	$$H - \overset{H}{\underset{H}{C}} - \overset{H}{\underset{H}{C}} - \overset{O}{C} - OH$$
Butanoic acid	C_3H_7COOH	$$H - \overset{H}{\underset{H}{C}} - \overset{H}{\underset{H}{C}} - \overset{H}{\underset{H}{C}} - \overset{O}{C} - OH$$ 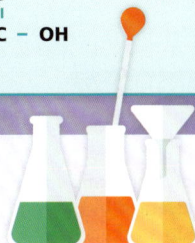

Properties of Carboxylic Acids

- They are weak acids – dissolving in water to produce H+ ions.
Because they are weak, only a small proportion of the molecules ionise.

- They react slowly with metal carbonates to form water, a salt and carbon dioxide.
The name of each salt ends in –oate. For example, methanoic acid forms methanoates, and ethanoic acid forms ethanoates.

- They react with alcohols to form esters. For example:

CH_3COOH	+	C_2H_5OH	⟹	$CH_3COOC_2H_5$	+	H_2O
Ethanoic acid		Ethanol		Ethyl ethanoate		Water

Esters

Esters are a homologous series of compounds with the functional group –COO–.
They are volatile chemicals, each with a distinctive smell. They occur naturally in fruit and often give a fruit its smell. They are used in perfumes and artificial flavourings.

Polymers & Polymerisation

Polymers are compounds made of a long chain of repeated 'units' called **monomers**. A polymer often consists of hundreds of monomers. All plastics are polymers, often containing alkene monomers. The process of polymer formation is called **polymerisation**.

Addition Polymerisation

In addition polymerisation reactions, many monomers join together to form polymers. Addition polymers are made from monomers with a C=C double bond (unsaturated compounds). The process requires heat, high pressure and a catalyst.

During addition polymerisation, the C=C bond opens up so the next monomer can be added. Nothing is removed in the reaction, so no other molecules are formed. For example, during the **polymerisation of ethene**, thousands of ethene molecules join together to make **poly(ethene)**.

Ethene monomers

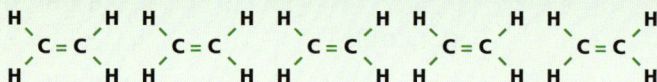

Heat + Pressure + Catalyst   **Polymerisation**

Polyethene

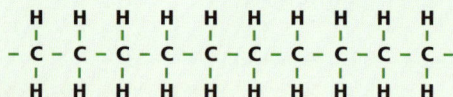

A polymer formula is too big to display in full. Instead, it is represented by placing the molecular formula for the repeating unit in brackets, with a subscript n.

The n represents the degree of polymerisation: the number of repeated units in the polymer. This is the formula for polyethene:

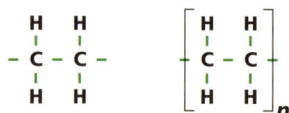

Repeating unit   **Structural formula**

Condensation Polymerisation

Condensation polymerisation involves monomers with different functional groups.

The monomers react, forming a bond and releasing a small molecule, usually water.

The example on the right shows the formation of a polyester by condensation polymerisation.

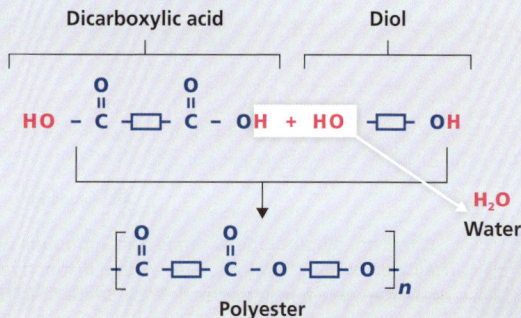

Dicarboxylic acid   **Diol**

$$HO - C - C - OH + HO - OH$$

H_2O
Water

Polyester

daydream
EDUCATION

Amino Acids & Naturally Occurring Polymers

Several important biological molecules, such as proteins, starch, cellulose and DNA, are naturally occurring polymers. Proteins are made of repeating units called amino acids.

Amino Acids

Amino acids are unusual molecules because they contain two functional groups: a basic amino group and an acidic carboxyl group. Only one part of the amino acid molecule varies. (About 20 different amino acids are found in living things).

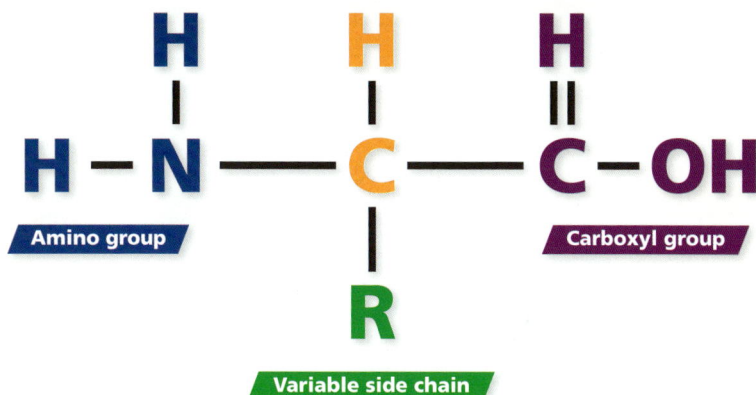

Amino group

Carboxyl group

Variable side chain

The letter R is used to symbolise the variable group because no chemical element has the symbol R.

If the amino group of one amino acid reacts with the carboxyl group of another, a bond forms through condensation polymerisation. For every new bond produced by this process, a water molecule is released.

The amino acids form a long-chain polymer known as a **polypeptide**.

Longer polymers are called **proteins**. Many different amino acids are combined in the same chain to produce proteins.

In the example to the right, a molecule of water is removed from two molecules of the amino acid glycine to form a peptide bond.

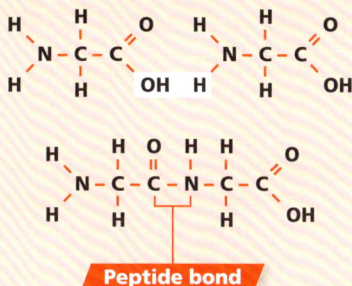

Peptide bond

Glucose Polymers

Glucose can act as a monomer to form different types of long-chain carbohydrate molecules. Two important glucose polymers in plants are starch, which acts as a food store, and cellulose, which forms the cell walls of plant cells.

DNA

Deoxyribonucleic acid, or DNA, is a vitally important, naturally occurring polymer. It is found in all living things, and it contains the chemical 'code' that controls the manufacture of all the proteins a cell needs. The monomer that makes up DNA is a **nucleotide**.

DNA Nucleotide Structure

There are four possible nitrogenous bases in a DNA nucleotide: adenine, thymine, guanine and cytosine.

Phosphate group

Nitrogenous base

Sugar

Nitrogenous bases

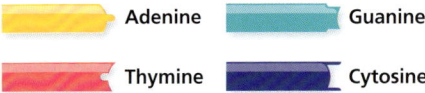

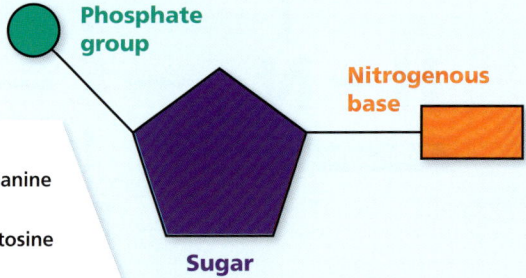

Adenine   Guanine

Thymine   Cytosine

DNA Structure

The DNA molecule consists of two chains of nucleotides that are wound into a spiral called a **double helix**. The chains are joined together by intermolecular forces between the bases called Hydrogen bonds.

The pairings of these nucleotide bases determine the coding for an organism's genes.

Adenine always pairs with thymine, and guanine with cytosine.

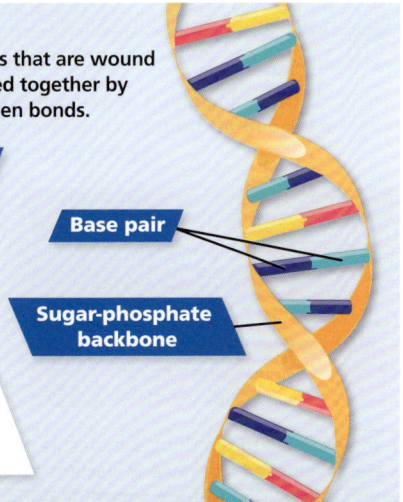

Base pair

Sugar-phosphate backbone

G always binds to **C**

Guanine   Cytosine

T always binds to **A**

Thymine   Adenine

daydream EDUCATION

Purity & Formulations

Pure Substances

In everyday language, *pure* often refers to a substance that has had nothing else added to it, but the 'substance' in this case is not necessarily a single element or compound (e.g. 'pure' milk). In chemistry, a pure substance is a single element or compound that has not been mixed with any other substance.

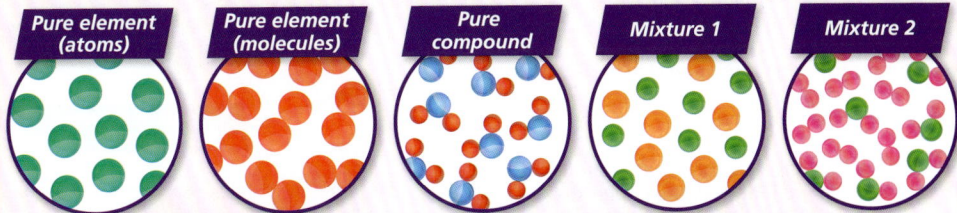

| Pure element (atoms) | Pure element (molecules) | Pure compound | Mixture 1 | Mixture 2 |

Pure elements and compounds have specific melting and boiling points.

If another substance is mixed in, the melting and boiling points will change. As a result, melting and boiling point data can be used to distinguish mixtures from pure substances. The purer the sample, the closer its melting and boiling points will be to those of the pure substance.

Example:

Methanol has a boiling point of 64.7°C. Three mixtures containing methanol are tested. Their boiling points are:

A 65.3°C   **B** 67.4°C   **C** 66.3°C

From this, we can determine that mixture A contains the least impurities because its boiling point is the nearest to that of pure methanol.

Formulations

A formulation is a mixture that has been designed as a useful substance. Formulations are made by mixing components in carefully measured quantities. This is necessary to ensure the formulation has the desired properties for its use.

Some common formulations:

Paint

Medicines

Fuels

Cleaning agents

Alloys

Manufactured food products

Fertilisers

daydream EDUCATION

Chromatography

Chromatography is a method for separating mixtures and identifying their components. There are various types of chromatography.

Separating and Identifying Substances in a Mixture

During chromatography, substances travel in two 'phases'. In paper chromatography, the **stationary phase** is the paper, and the **mobile phase** is the solvent.

How long each substance spends in each phase varies depending on its attraction to the paper and the solvent.

Substances that have a stronger attraction to the paper spend longer in the paper (the stationary phase) and move more slowly, only travelling a short distance up the paper.

More soluble substances, which have a stronger attraction to the solvent, spend longer in the mobile phase and move more quickly, travelling further up the paper.

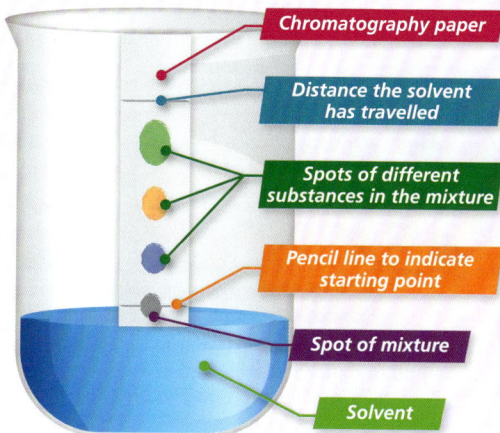

Chromatography paper

Distance the solvent has travelled

Spots of different substances in the mixture

Pencil line to indicate starting point

Spot of mixture

Solvent

In the example above, the blue substance has spent the longest time in the stationary phase, so it has moved the shortest distance. This means that it has a strong attraction to the paper.

Conversely, the green substance has spent the longest time in the mobile phase, so it has moved the farthest. This means that it has a strong attraction to the solvent.

R_f Values

The R_f value is the ratio of the distance moved by the dissolved substance to the distance moved by the solvent.

$$R_f = \frac{\text{distance travelled by substance}}{\text{distance travelled by solvent}}$$

Different compounds have different R_f values in a specific solvent. Therefore, the R_f can be used to identify the components (compounds) in a mixture.

Uses of Chromatography Recap

Separating Mixtures — Chromatography is used to separate mixtures. It is easiest to separate coloured mixtures, but methods are available that can identify transparent 'spots'.

Testing Purity — Compounds in a mixture may separate depending on the solvent, but a pure substance produces only one spot in all solvents.

Identifying Substances — It is possible to identify different compounds using their R_f value.

daydream EDUCATION

Identification of Common Gases

Test for Hydrogen

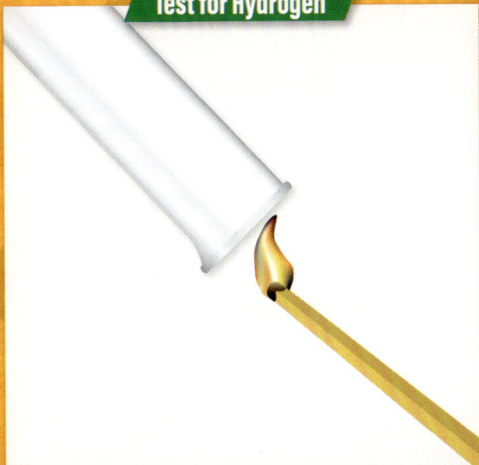

A burning splint is held at the mouth of a test tube of the gas. Hydrogen burns rapidly with a characteristic 'squeaky pop'.

Test for Oxygen

A glowing splint is inserted into the gas to be tested. If oxygen is present, the splint will re-light.

Test for Carbon Dioxide

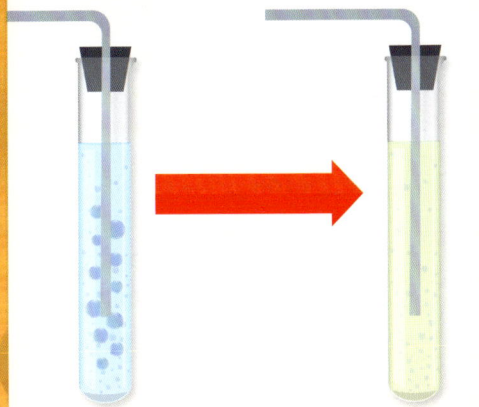

The gas to be tested is shaken with or bubbled through limewater (calcium hydroxide). If carbon dioxide is present, the limewater will turn cloudy or milky due to the formation of insoluble calcium carbonate.

Test for Chlorine

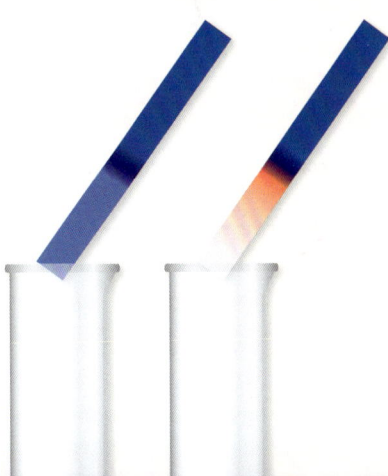

Damp blue litmus paper is placed into the gas to be tested. Chlorine will briefly turn the paper red and then bleach it white.

daydream EDUCATION

Identifying Ions

Chemical tests and **spectroscopic** tests (related to the emission of light) – are used to identify specific ions.

Flame Test

A flame test can be used to identify some metal ions. The compound being tested is held in a Bunsen flame, and the colour of the flame produced indicates the metal ion present.

In this image, the flame test shows the presence of sodium ions.

Metal	Ion	Flame Colour
Lithium	Li^+	Crimson
Sodium	Na^+	Yellow
Potassium	K^+	Lilac
Calcium	Ca^{2+}	Orange-red
Copper	Cu^{2+}	Green

With a sample containing a mix of ions, it may be difficult to identify those ions based on flame colour.

Sodium Hydroxide Test

Sodium hydroxide can be used to test for metal ions with insoluble hydroxides. The metal ions react with sodium hydroxide to form metal hydroxide precipitates.

$$CuSO_{4\,(aq)} \ + \ 2NaOH_{(aq)} \ \longrightarrow \ Na_2SO_{4\,(aq)} \ + \ Cu(OH)_{(s)}$$

Copper sulfate   Sodium hydroxide   Sodium sulfate   Copper hydroxide

The colour of the precipitate formed can be used to identify the metal involved in the reaction. The precipitate colours formed by different metal ions are shown below.

Metal	Ion	Precipitate Colour	Ionic Equation
Aluminium	Al^{3+}	White *	$Al^{3+}_{(aq)} + 3OH^-_{(aq)} \longrightarrow Al(OH)_{3\,(s)}$
Calcium	Ca^{2+}	White *	$Ca^{2+}_{(aq)} + 2OH^-_{(aq)} \longrightarrow Ca(OH)_{2\,(s)}$
Magnesium	Mg^{2+}	White *	$Mg^{2+}_{(aq)} + 2OH^-_{(aq)} \longrightarrow Mg(OH)_{2\,(s)}$
Copper	Cu^{2+}	Blue	$Cu^{2+}_{(aq)} + 2OH^-_{(aq)} \longrightarrow Cu(OH)_{2\,(s)}$
Iron (II)	Fe^{2+}	Green	$Fe^{2+}_{(aq)} + 2OH^-_{(aq)} \longrightarrow Fe(OH)_{2\,(s)}$
Iron (III)	Fe^{3+}	Brown	$Fe^{3+}_{(aq)} + 3OH^-_{(aq)} \longrightarrow Fe(OH)_{3\,(s)}$

The ionic equations show the ions involved in precipitate formation. Spectator ions (Na^+ from NaOH and the anion from the metal compound) are not included.

* The precipitates formed by calcium, magnesium and aluminium all look similar. However, if excess sodium hydroxide solution is added, the aluminium hydroxide precipitate dissolves to form a colourless solution. Calcium and magnesium ions can be distinguished by using a flame test.

daydream
EDUCATION

Tests for Negative Ions

Carbonates

Carbonates can be identified based on how they react to dilute acids, such as hydrochloric acid. Specifically, they release CO_2, which creates a fizz and turns lime water cloudy.

Example

$$2HCl_{(aq)} + Na_2CO_{3\,(aq)} \rightarrow 2NaCl_{(aq)} + CO_{2\,(g)} + H_2O_{(l)}$$

Hydrochloric acid   Sodium carbonate   Sodium chlorine   Carbon dioxide   Water

Halides

Halides can be identified by adding dilute nitric acid, followed by silver nitrate solution. Halide ions produce a precipitate, with the colour indicating which halide is present:

Chloride ions: white   **Bromide ions: cream**   **Iodide ions: yellow**

Example

$$NaCl_{(aq)} + AgNO_{3\,(aq)} \rightarrow NaNO_{3\,(aq)} + AgCl_{(s)}$$

Sodium chloride   Silver nitrate   Sodium nitrate   Silver chloride

Sulfates

Sulfates can be identified by adding dilute hydrochloric acid and then barium chloride solution. A white precipitate (barium sulfate) indicates the presence of a sulfate.

Example

$$K_2SO_{4\,(aq)} + BaCl_{2\,(aq)} \rightarrow 2KCl_{(aq)} + BaSO_{4\,(s)}$$

Potassium sulfate   Barium chloride   Potassium chloride   Barium sulfate

Instrumental Methods   Elements and compounds can be detected and identified by using instrumental methods, which are accurate, sensitive and rapid.

Flame Emission Spectroscopy

Flame emission spectroscopy is used to analyse metal ions in solutions.

A sample is heated in a flame. The light produced by the flames passes through a **spectroscope**. The spectroscope's output is a **line spectrum**, showing the different wavelengths in the light.

The spectrum indicates which metal ions are present; each ion has its own individual line spectrum. The intensities of the wavelengths reflect the concentrations of each ion.

The line spectrum for three metal ions (A, B and C) are shown opposite along with a line spectrum for an unknown sample.

A comparison of the line spectrums indicates that the unknown sample contains ion C but not ions A or B.

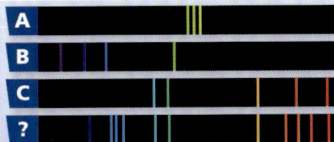

Spectroscopy is an improvement over previous tests because it is quantitative – that is, it measures each ion's concentration rather than merely indicating its presence. It is also much more sensitive, enabling it to detect ions in minute quantities.

daydream EDUCATION

The Earth's Atmosphere

Argon 0.9%　　Other 0.1%

Oxygen 21%

Nitrogen 78%

The Proportion of Gases in the Atmosphere

The Earth's atmosphere is dynamic and constantly changing. However, the proportion of gases in the atmosphere has been roughly the same for the last 200 million years.

Nitrogen and oxygen make up approximately 99% of the Earth's atmosphere. Other gases include carbon dioxide, water vapour and noble gases.

The Early Atmosphere

The proportion of gases in the atmosphere was different when the Earth was first formed. Theories of what was in Earth's early atmosphere have changed over time, and evidence is limited because the Earth was formed over 4.6 billion years ago.

When the Earth formed, its first atmosphere would have been made of hydrogen and helium, but these low-density gases would have quickly drifted into space. The chart below shows one theory of how our atmosphere formed.

Stage	Events	Atmosphere
1	Intense volcanic activity produced gases and water vapour.	Carbon dioxide, water vapour, ammonia, methane and very little oxygen (similar to the current atmospheres of Mars and Venus)
2	The Earth continued to cool, and water vapour in the atmosphere condensed to form oceans. Carbon dioxide dissolved in the water, and carbonates were precipitated, producing sediments. Early plant life evolved.	Mostly carbon dioxide; some water vapour, nitrogen and ammonia
3	Early forms of plant life emerged, which used carbon dioxide to form oxygen through photosynthesis. Some of the oxygen reacted with ammonia to form nitrogen.	Current atmosphere, including nitrogen and oxygen

daydream EDUCATION

How Oxygen Increased

Oxygen started to be produced on Earth about 2.7 billion years ago, with the appearance of algae and plants, which carry out photosynthesis.

Photosynthesis is the process by which plants, algae and other organisms produce their own food (glucose). It uses light energy, carbon dioxide and water to produce glucose and oxygen. It can be represented by this equation:

$$6CO_2 + 6H_2O \longrightarrow C_6H_{12}O_6 + 6O_2$$

carbon dioxide + water $\xrightarrow{\text{light}}$ glucose + oxygen

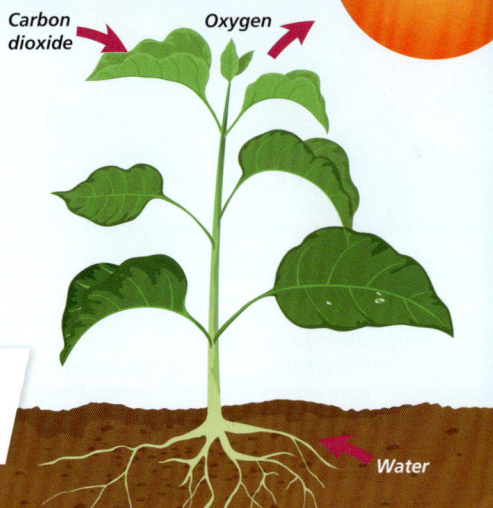

Carbon dioxide → → ← *Oxygen*

Water

Over the next billion years more plants evolved, and the percentage of oxygen in the atmosphere increased sufficiently to allow animal life to develop and evolve.

How Carbon Dioxide Decreased

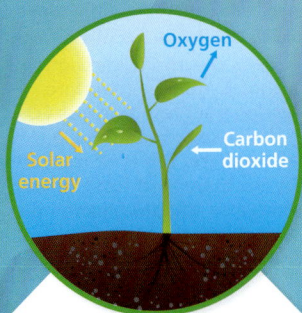

Oxygen

Solar energy

Carbon dioxide

The formation of oxygen by photosynthesis also leads to a decrease in the percentage of carbon dioxide in the atmosphere.

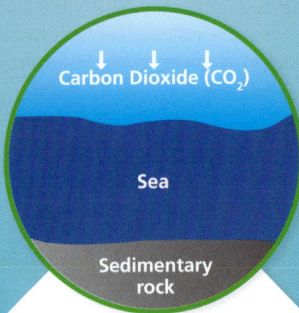

Carbon Dioxide (CO_2)

Sea

Sedimentary rock

Large amounts of carbon dioxide also dissolved in the oceans, forming sediments (precipitates) which gave rise to sedimentary rocks (e.g. limestone – calcium carbonate).

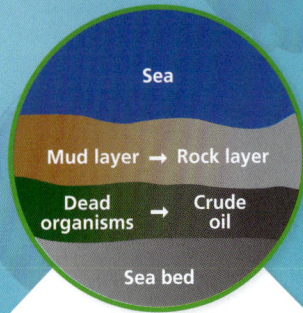

Sea

Mud layer → Rock layer

Dead organisms → Crude oil

Sea bed

The dead bodies of microscopic plants became compressed by this rock formation and were converted into fossil fuels – coal, oil and gas.

daydream EDUCATION

Greenhouse Gases

Greenhouse gases (including water vapour, carbon dioxide and methane) absorb infrared radiation from the Sun and keep the Earth warm enough to sustain life.

The Greenhouse Effect

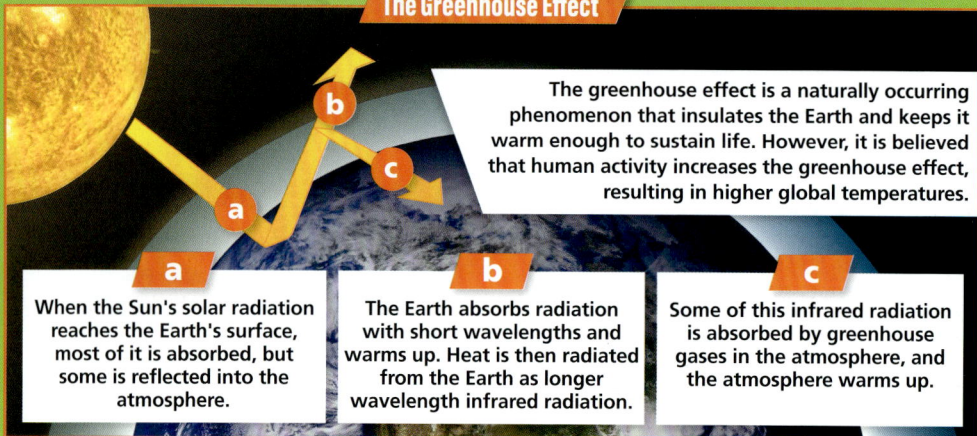

The greenhouse effect is a naturally occurring phenomenon that insulates the Earth and keeps it warm enough to sustain life. However, it is believed that human activity increases the greenhouse effect, resulting in higher global temperatures.

a
When the Sun's solar radiation reaches the Earth's surface, most of it is absorbed, but some is reflected into the atmosphere.

b
The Earth absorbs radiation with short wavelengths and warms up. Heat is then radiated from the Earth as longer wavelength infrared radiation.

c
Some of this infrared radiation is absorbed by greenhouse gases in the atmosphere, and the atmosphere warms up.

The Effect of Human Activity on Greenhouse Gas Levels

A number of human activities are thought to play a role in the increase in the greenhouse gases methane and carbon dioxide in the atmosphere.

Fossil Fuels

Fossil fuels such as oil, gas and coal are burnt to generate energy for transportation, manufacturing and electricity production. However, the process of burning fossil fuels releases CO_2 into the atmosphere and is the main source of greenhouse gas emissions.

Agriculture

Agriculture, especially livestock and rice farming, produces huge amounts of the greenhouse gas methane. It is released by animals during digestion and by matter decomposed by microbes in flooded rice paddy fields.

Deforestation

Trees absorb CO_2 through photosynthesis. Therefore, clearing trees results in less CO_2 being removed from the atmosphere. This is worsened by the burning of fossil fuels, which also releases greenhouse gases into the atmosphere.

Based on peer-reviewed evidence, many scientists believe that human activities have caused, and will continue to cause, the temperature of the atmosphere to rise, resulting in global climate change. However, not everyone agrees with this theory.

The atmosphere is a very complex system, so it is not easy to produce an accurate model that everyone can understand. This has several consequences:

Simplified models do not fully explain the theory and therefore may be misleading.

Speculation and media reports may only present parts of the evidence.

Some opinions may be biased (e.g. those from industries that produce greenhouse gases).

daydream EDUCATION

Effects of Climate Change

Climate change has a significant effect on both the environment and people.

Warmer global temperatures will cause glaciers and ice sheets to melt, leading to rising sea levels and the loss of polar habitats.

Rising sea levels will result in low-lying coastal areas flooding more frequently or even becoming permanently submerged in water.

Many plant and animal species are at risk of becoming extinct as their habitats are altered or damaged by climate change. For example, many of the world's coral reefs, which support a diverse range of marine life, are at risk of bleaching and destruction due to rising sea temperatures.

Warmer temperatures and higher sea levels will lead to more extreme weather events and a change in precipitation patterns.

Although agriculture in some areas may benefit from warmer temperatures, many areas will become hotter and drier. This will result in drought, desertification, declining crop yields and food and water shortages.

The Carbon Footprint

A carbon footprint is the total amount of carbon dioxide and other greenhouse gases emitted over the full life cycle of a product, service or event. Carbon footprints can be reduced by decreasing carbon dioxide and methane emissions. Examples include:

Alternative Energy Production: This includes energy sources, such as hydroelectric power and solar power, which have lower greenhouse gas emissions than burning fossil fuels.

Energy Conservation: Energy use and greenhouse gas emissions can be reduced by using energy-efficient devices and appliances.

Recycling: Using recycled and recyclable materials can reduce the amount of fossil fuels required to create new materials.

Reducing Deforestation & Planting Trees: The increase in greenhouse gas emissions from burning fossil fuels can be offset by reducing deforestation rates and planting trees, which absorb carbon dioxide.

Carbon Capture & Storage: This involves capturing carbon dioxide released by industry or burning fossil fuels and then storing it safely underground.

There are some difficulties in reducing carbon footprints:

Many countries rely on fossil fuels for their economic prosperity, so it is against their interests to cease production and use.

Alternative energy sources can be costly and do not produce as much energy as burning fossil fuels.

Measures may require lifestyle changes (e.g. recycling and reducing car use), which some people are unwilling to make.

daydream
EDUCATION

Atmospheric Pollution

The Earth's atmosphere has become polluted in a variety of ways by human activity.

Pollution from Fuels

Most fuels are carbon based, although many also contain hydrogen, sulfur and nitrogen compounds.

During the combustion of fuels, the compounds react with oxygen to become oxidised. As a result, several gases are released into the atmosphere.

Complete Combustion of Hydrocarbon Fuels

Carbon dioxide and water vapour are released by the complete combustion of hydrocarbon fuels.

hydrocarbon + oxygen ➡ carbon dioxide + water

Carbon dioxide and water vapour are greenhouse gases, which many people believe contribute to global warming and climate change.

Incomplete Combustion of Hydrocarbon Fuels

When there is not enough oxygen for complete combustion of hydrocarbon fuels, particles of carbon (soot) and carbon monoxide can also be released.

hydrocarbon + oxygen ➡ carbon dioxide + carbon monoxide + carbon + water

Carbon monoxide is a dangerous gas because it is highly toxic. It is also colourless and odourless, which makes it difficult to detect.

Carbon can also be released as small particles of unburnt hydrocarbons known as soot. These particles can cause health problems in humans and global dimming.

Health Problems

Particles of soot can be inhaled, causing respiratory problems, including coronary heart disease, asthma, bronchitis and cancer.

Global Dimming

Particles of soot in the atmosphere can block sunlight, reducing the amount of light reaching the surface of the Earth.

Sulfur Dioxide and Oxides of Nitrogen

Sulfur dioxide and nitrogen oxides also cause atmospheric pollution.

Sulfur dioxide is released due to sulfur impurities in many hydrocarbon fuels such as coal. Nitrogen oxides form at high temperatures when oxygen and nitrogen in the air react.

Both products can cause respiratory problems and acid rain. Acid rain is created when the products dissolve in water vapour in clouds to form sulfuric and nitric acids.

daydream EDUCATION

The Earth's Resources

All resources essential for human development – from oxygen in the air we breathe to food, water, fuel, clothing and building materials – are all sourced from the Earth.

Earth's resources provide:

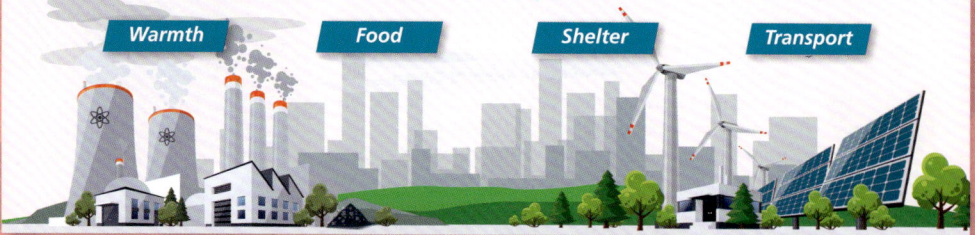

Warmth **Food** **Shelter** **Transport**

Non-Renewable Resources

These resources are finite and will eventually run out. Once they are depleted, they cannot be replenished.

Renewable Resources

These resources are infinite. They can be easily replenished and will not run out.

Sustainable development is development that meets the needs of the present without compromising the ability of future generations to meet their own needs.

The Six Rs of Sustainable Development

Rethink — Think before you buy or use products.

Refuse — Do not use products that are environmentally unsustainable.

Repair — Fix or repair items rather than throwing them away.

Reduce — Limit the amount of resources you use.

Reuse — Find new uses for old objects instead of throwing them away.

Recycle — Recycle what you can, and use recycled materials when possible.

daydream EDUCATION

Recycling Materials

Metal, glass, plastic and building materials are usually made from limited raw materials. To reduce the usage of these materials and to ensure that they last long, they can be reused or recycled.

Although recycling can be expensive and require lots of energy, it generally requires less energy and generates less pollution than mining and extraction. It also reduces damage to the environment and landscape.

Metals

Metals can be recycled by melting them down and making them into something new. This means mining and the pollution caused by it are reduced, finite resources are conserved and there is less waste.

Glass

Glass can often be reused. Alternatively, if it is separated by colour and chemical composition, it can be crushed and melted to make new products.

The Role of Chemistry in Sustainable Development

Chemistry can improve agricultural and industrial processes and lead to new products that can aid sustainable development. Examples include:

- The use of catalysts to speed up chemical reactions so that they require less energy input

- The development and use of carbon nanotubes to strengthen materials and extend their life

- Researching conditions that make manufacturing processes more efficient

- Developing pesticides that break down and so do not enter food chains or pollute the environment

- Developing 'smart' materials that can be added to soil to retain water

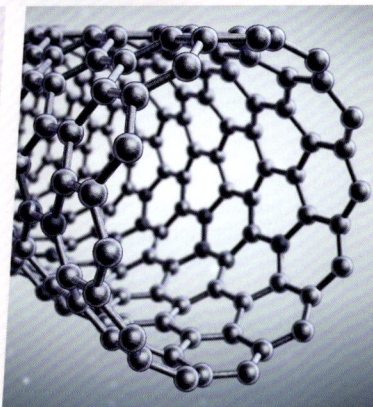

Potable Water

Water is essential for life. It is used for drinking, washing, sanitation, cooking, and industrial and manufacturing processes.

Potable water is water that is safe to drink. It is not pure water – it contains dissolved substances, including a safe level of dissolved salts and microbes. After use, waste water must be treated before being released back into the environment.

Local conditions and the availability of water supplies determine how potable water is produced.

UK Potable Water Supply

In the UK, water is sourced from rain that has gathered in groundwater stores, rivers, lakes and reservoirs. It has a low level of dissolved substances but still needs to be treated before it is safe to drink.

Treatment often consists of three stages:

1 The water is allowed to settle. Large soil particles settle to the bottom, and the water is drawn from the top.

2 The water is passed through filter beds, which filter out smaller particles.

3 The filtered water is then sterilised to remove most bacteria. The sterilising agents include chlorine, ozone and ultraviolet light.

Some countries do not have a sufficient supply of freshwater. Potable water can also be obtained from seawater by a process of desalination.

Desalination can be done by distillation or by processes that use membranes (e.g. reverse osmosis), but these processes require large amounts of energy and are expensive.

Heat the mixture until the substance with the lowest boiling point starts to boil and turn into a gas.

The gas cools, condenses in the condenser and collects in the beaker. The rest of the mixture remains in the flask.

Make sure you heat the solution to the boiling point of only one of the substances. If you heat the solution to a temperature at which both substances boil, they will become mixed again.

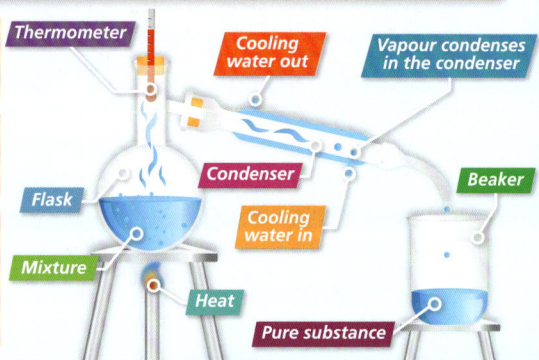

Thermometer
Cooling water out
Vapour condenses in the condenser
Condenser
Flask
Cooling water in
Beaker
Mixture
Heat
Pure substance

daydream EDUCATION

Waste Water Treatment

After use, waste water must be treated before being released back into the environment. Potable water is a limited resource so it must be recycled for reuse where possible. Waste water comes from several sources.

Domestic Use	Water is used in the home for cleaning, washing and flushing away wastes. Sewage needs to be treated to remove harmful bacteria and organic matter.
Agriculture	Water is used in agriculture for irrigation (watering crops). Waste water, which often contains pesticides and fertilisers, drains into streams and rivers.
Industry	Most water extracted from freshwater sources is used for energy production. It is also used for manufacturing. Waste water from industry needs to be treated to remove organic matter and harmful chemicals including oil.

Sewage Treatment

Sewage treatment cleans waste water to make it fit for drinking.

1 Screening
Large sediment and grit is removed, and the sewage is passed to a sedimentation tank.

2 Sedimentation
The sewage is left to settle so heavy sediment sinks to the bottom and lighter effluent floats to the top.

3 Aerobic Treatment
The effluent is drained into an aeration tank where it is pumped with air. Good bacteria breaks down harmful bacteria through aerobic digestion.

4 Release
The treated water is released back into the environment.

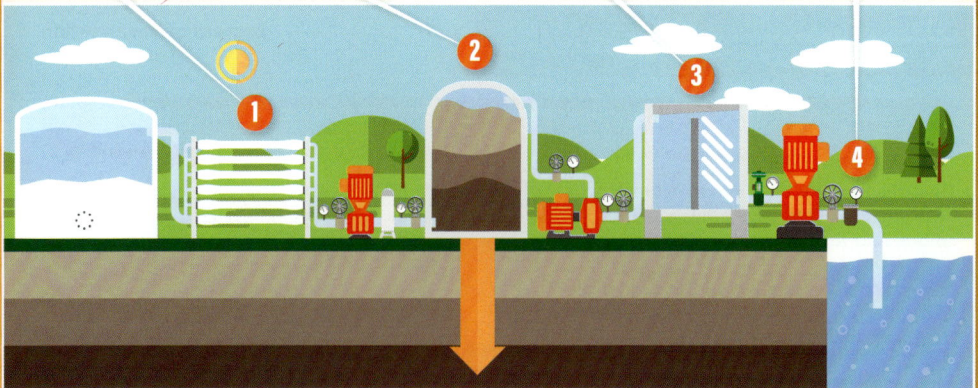

During anaerobic digestion, the bacteria produce methane, which can be burned and used as an energy source.

The heavy sediment (sludge) is moved to a separate tank where it is broken down anaerobically by bacteria.

The digested waste can be used as fertiliser.

daydream EDUCATION

Alternative Methods of Metal Extraction

Most metals are found in rocks called ores and have to be extracted from these ores through mining. Due to their over-extraction, the Earth's resources of metal ores are diminishing.

Some metals, such as copper, have become so scarce that low-grade ores, which contain a small percentage of copper, are having to be mined through new methods of extraction.

Phytomining

Phytomining is used to extract copper from soil that is rich in copper compounds.

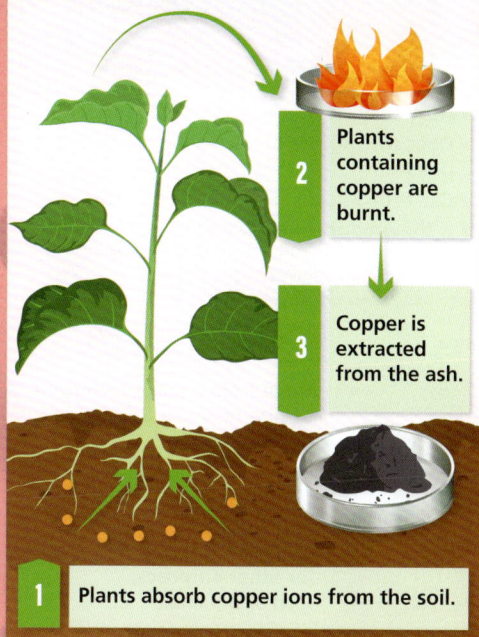

2 Plants containing copper are burnt.

3 Copper is extracted from the ash.

1 Plants absorb copper ions from the soil.

Bioleaching

Bioleaching uses bacteria that absorb copper compounds to produce solutions called leachates, which contain copper compounds.

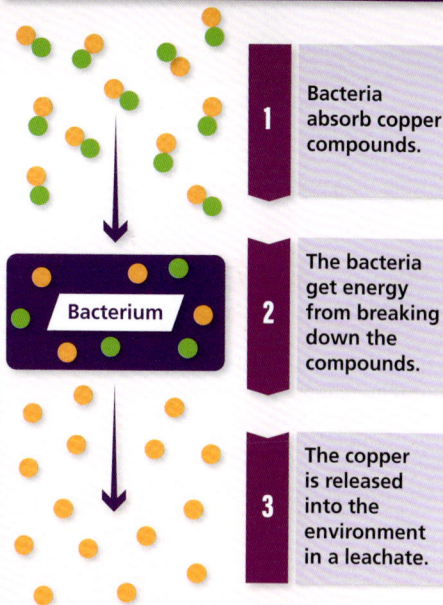

1 Bacteria absorb copper compounds.

Bacterium

2 The bacteria get energy from breaking down the compounds.

3 The copper is released into the environment in a leachate.

After phytomining and bioleaching, the copper can be extracted from the ash or the leachate. Extraction is done through a **displacement** reaction using scrap iron (because iron is more reactive than copper) or by **electrolysis**.

Environmental Benefits

Neither phytomining nor bioleaching involves traditional mining practices such as digging or moving and disposing of large amounts of rock. Therefore, they are better for the environment.

daydream EDUCATION

Life Cycle Assessment

Life cycle assessments (LCAs) are used to assess the environmental impacts of every stage of a product's life (including disposal).

1 Extraction & Processing

- Does extraction and processing damage the environment and cause pollution?
- Does extracting the material require large amounts of energy and create lots of waste?

2 Manufacturing & Packaging

- Does the manufacturing process use large amounts of energy, cause pollution or produce harmful waste products?
- Does the packaging create a lot of waste?
- Can the packaging be recycled?

3 Use & Operation

- Does the product damage the environment?
- Does the product require lots of energy to run?
- How long is the product's lifecycle?

4 Product Disposal

- How easy is it to dispose of the product?
- Does the process of disposal result in pollution?
- Can it be reused or recycled after use?
- Is the product biodegradable?

Evaluating the Sustainability of Using Paper and Plastic Bags

Paper Bags	LCA Stage	Plastic Bags
Made from sustainable trees, but require large amounts of energy to produce	Extraction and Processing	Made from crude oil, which is a finite resource
Total energy use: **2,622 MJ** Freshwater usage: **1,004 gal**	Manufacturing and Packaging (figures based on 1,000 bags)	Total energy use: **763 MJ** Freshwater usage: **58 gal**
Not very strong and do not last very long Not waterproof	Use and Operation	Can be reused as a bag and for other purposes, such as bin liners
Biodegradable and can be recycled	Product Disposal	Not biodegradable but can be recycled Often end up in landfill

Each type of bag has benefits and drawbacks, so a judgement must be made on which benefits are most important. It is not always possible or easy to quantify figures in an LCA. Figures are often biased because they are based on value judgements.

Sometimes LCAs can be misused. Selective or shortened LCAs can be presented (e.g. in advertising) so as to reach predetermined and preferred conclusions.

daydream EDUCATION

Corrosion & Its Prevention

What Is Corrosion?

Corrosion is the destruction of materials by chemical reactions with substances in the environment (usually oxygen). Some metals are more reactive than others and corrode faster.

Iron corrodes easily to form iron (III) oxide, or rust, which is an example of corrosion. Rust is specific to iron and does not result when other metals corrode.

Only the surface of iron reacts with chemicals in the environment. However, as rust is powdery, it is easily removed to expose a new surface, which can also rust. Thus, iron can rust away over time.

For rust to form, water and oxygen are needed. This can be shown by an experiment in which an iron nail is placed in three conditions: air and water, water only and air only.

In test tube B, boiling the water has removed the oxygen, and the oil prevents the water from absorbing more.

In test tube C, anhydrous calcium chloride absorbs water from the atmosphere.

The iron nail rusts only in test tube A.

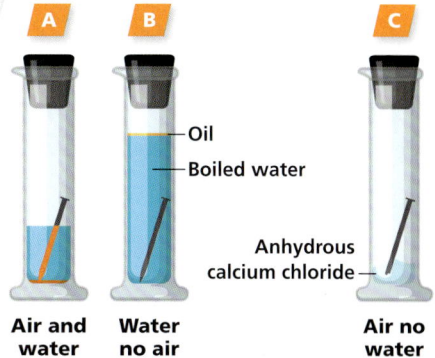

A — Air and water

B — Water no air — Oil — Boiled water

C — Air no water — Anhydrous calcium chloride

Aluminium also corrodes in air. However, no significant corrosion occurs because aluminium oxide forms a protective layer that sticks to the metal, sealing the metal from the air.

Preventing Corrosion

Iron and steel, an alloy of iron, can be protected from rust by:

- **Applying a protective coating,** such as paint, grease or plastic. This acts as a barrier that seals the metal from the air. Using electrolysis to coat the metal with another metal, or electroplating, also offers protection.

- **Sacrificial protection.** A more reactive metal (usually zinc) is attached to the iron. Oxygen and water react with the more reactive metal rather than the iron.

- **Galvanising.** A coating of zinc is added to iron to provide a protective barrier. However, if it chips, the zinc still provides sacrificial protection. Galvanised iron is often used for buckets and outdoor nails.

Alloys

Alloys are mixtures of metals or metals and other elements, such as carbon. Metals are alloyed to improve their physical properties.

Useful Alloys

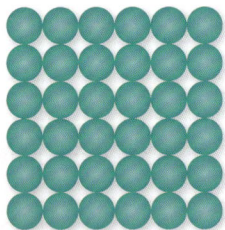

Metals have a structure of regular layers of atoms. Therefore, pure metals tend to be soft and malleable because the layers can easily slide over each other.

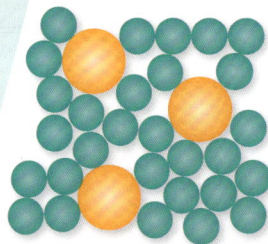

Adding **another element** to a pure metal disrupts its regular structure and makes it harder and stronger.

Steel

Pure iron is too soft and brittle to be used on its own, so it is alloyed with carbon and other metals to make steel. Different types of steel have specific amounts of these elements.

0.01–0.30% carbon	0.6–1.5% carbon	Minimum of 10.5% chromium
Easily shaped and tough Inexpensive but rusts easily	Very hard but brittle Prone to rust	Tough, hard and strong Highly resistant to corrosion

Bronze
Bronze is an alloy of tin and copper. Alloying copper, which is soft and used for decorative purposes, with tin makes it harder and more resistant to corrosion. Bronze is used in statues and sculptures.

Brass
Brass is an alloy of copper and zinc. It is highly resistant to corrosion and is used in taps, door handles and musical instruments.

Aluminium Alloys
Aluminium is durable, lightweight and resistant to corrosion. It has a low density but is not very strong. Therefore, it is often alloyed with other metals, such as copper and zinc, to create strong but lightweight materials.

Gold Alloys
Gold is mainly used to make jewellery. Adding copper, zinc or silver makes gold harder and changes its colour. The proportion of gold in an alloy is measured in carats, with 24 carat being 100% (pure) gold and 18 carat being 75% gold.

daydream
EDUCATION

Polymers, Ceramics & Composites

Polymers, ceramics and composites are useful materials made by chemical reactions.

Polymers

The properties of polymers depend on what monomers they are made from and the conditions under which they are made.

Low-density polyethene (LDPE) and high-density polyethene (HDPE) are both produced from ethene, but their properties vary due to the different conditions under which they are made.

LDPE

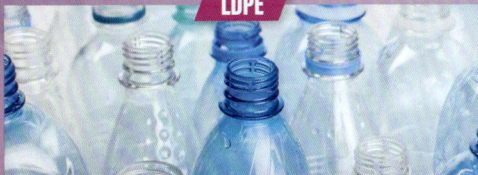

LDPE is made by the polymerisation of ethene under high pressure.

The polymer chains in LDPE are highly branched, so there are weak intermolecular forces of attraction between molecules. Therefore, LDPE is softer and more flexible than HDPE.

Uses: plastic bags and bottles

HDPE

HDPE is made by the polymerisation of ethene under low pressure.

Compared to the polymer chains in LDPE, those in HDPE are more linear and thus closer together, resulting in stronger intermolecular forces and a more crystalline structure. Therefore, HDPE is harder and more rigid than LDPE.

Uses: buckets, bins and drinks bottles

Thermosoftening Polymers

Thermosoftening polymers contain few cross-links between polymer chains, so they can be easily melted and re-shaped.

They are recyclable but cannot be used at high temperatures because they melt.

Examples include acrylic, high-impact polystyrene, LDPE, HDPE and polyvinyl chloride (PVC).

Thermosetting Polymers

Thermosetting polymers contain lots of cross-links between polymer chains. During formation, they undergo a chemical change that makes them permanently rigid and resistant to heat and fire.

They cannot be reformed and are not recyclable.

Examples include epoxy resin, polyester resin and urea formaldehyde.

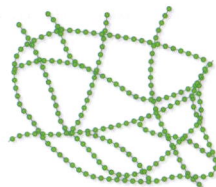

Ceramics

Ceramics are solid materials that have high melting points. They are made of non-metals but do not contain carbon.

Glass

Glass is a very hard but brittle non-crystalline ceramic. The most common form of glass is soda-lime glass, which is made from sand, limestone and sodium carbonate.

Although soda-lime glass has a high melting point, the melting point of borosilicate glass is even higher. Made from sand and boron trioxide, borosilicate glass is used to make glass cookware.

Clay Ceramics

Clay ceramics are used to make pottery, bricks and bathroom furniture (baths, sinks and toilets). They are made by shaping wet clay and then heating it in a furnace.

Clay ceramics make good insulators and are resistant to chemicals, but they are brittle. They are also hard, but not as hard as glass.

Composites

Composites are usually made from two materials: a matrix (binder) and a reinforcement. The matrix surrounds and binds together the fragments or fibres of the reinforcement. A composite has enhanced properties that neither constituent material has on its own.

Glass-Ceramic

Glass and clay ceramics are combined to create a composite that is hard but less brittle than the constituent materials.

Fibreglass

Glass fibres are embedded in a polymer (plastic) matrix to create a strong, low-density composite. It also has good thermal insulating properties, so it is often used in building insulation.

Concrete

Sand and gravel (aggregate) are embedded in cement and water to create, once hardened, a very strong composite material that is often used in construction. Embedding fibres can further reinforce concrete and reduce cracking and shrinkage during hardening.

The Haber Process

The Haber process is an industrial process in which nitrogen and hydrogen are reacted to form ammonia, a compound used in chemical fertilisers and cleaning products.

The reaction in the Haber process is reversible:

$$N_{2(g)} + 3H_{2(g)} \rightleftharpoons 2NH_{3(g)}$$

Nitrogen   **Hydrogen**   **Ammonia**

In the Haber process, nitrogen (from air) and hydrogen (from natural gas) are purified and passed over an iron catalyst at a high temperature (approx. 450°C) and high pressure (approx. 200 atmospheres).

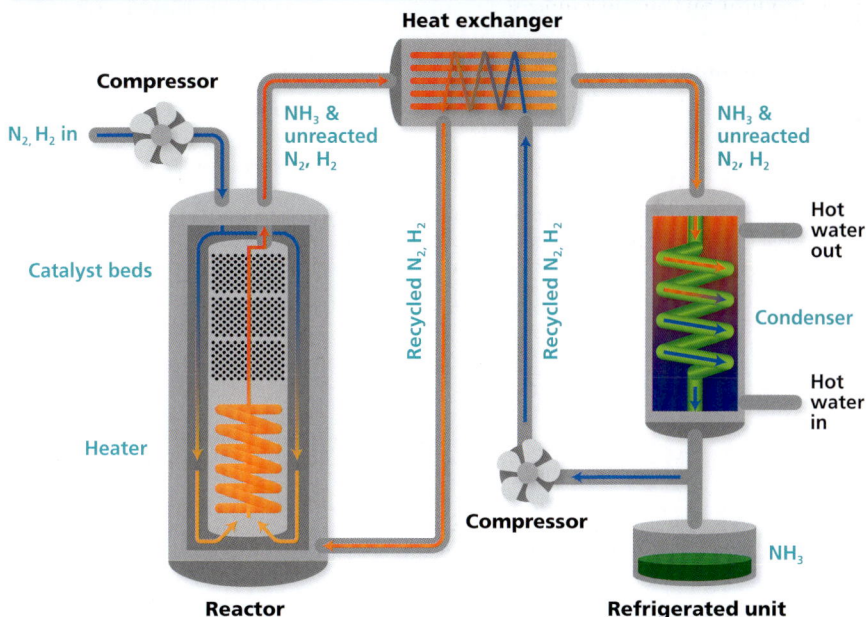

Heat exchanger

Compressor

N_2, H_2 in

NH_3 & unreacted N_2, H_2

NH_3 & unreacted N_2, H_2

Catalyst beds

Recycled N_2, H_2

Recycled N_2, H_2

Hot water out

Condenser

Hot water in

Heater

Compressor

NH_3

Reactor

Refrigerated unit

Because the reaction is reversible, some of the ammonia breaks down again into nitrogen and hydrogen. The efficiency of the reaction is only about 15%.

To improve efficiency, the mixture is cooled to condense the ammonia. The unused nitrogen and hydrogen are then recycled back into the reactor.

Dynamic Equilibrium & the Haber Process

The rate of a reaction depends on various factors, such as temperature, pressure and concentration of the reactants and products. However, these factors can also affect the dynamic equilibrium of the reaction, sometimes causing an opposite effect on the yield. In such instances, there must be a trade-off between increasing the rate of a reaction and maximising the yield.

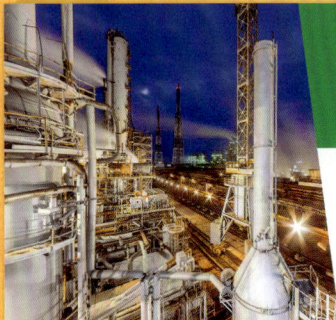

For example, as temperature increases so does the rate of a reaction. However, the formation of ammonia is **exothermic**, so an increase in temperature shifts the equilibrium to favour the breakdown of the ammonia into nitrogen and hydrogen.

For the reaction to occur at an optimum level, a compromise between the rate of the reaction and maximum yield is needed. For the Haber process to proceed at a commercially viable rate, the temperature must be 450°C. The nitrogen and hydrogen are also recycled to maintain their relatively high concentrations.

The total number of nitrogen and hydrogen molecules is greater than the number of ammonia molecules in the reaction.

$$N_{2(g)} + 3H_{2(g)} \rightleftharpoons 2NH_{3(g)}$$

Therefore, higher pressure shifts the position of equilibrium towards the products, increasing the yield of ammonia. Also, as pressure increases so does the rate of the reaction.

Creating high pressure can be dangerous and expensive. Therefore, both the costs and benefits must be considered when setting the pressure.

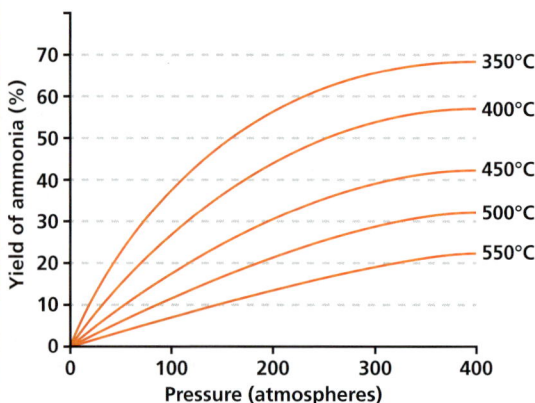

Graph axes: Yield of ammonia (%) from 0 to 70; Pressure (atmospheres) from 0 to 400. Curves labelled 350°C, 400°C, 450°C, 500°C, 550°C.

The graph above shows how pressure and temperature affect the yield of ammonia.

The iron catalyst used in the Haber process speeds up the reaction but has no effect on its direction. This means that the ammonia will be produced more quickly when the equilibrium favours it, although the actual yield is unaffected.

daydream EDUCATION

NPK Fertilisers

NPK fertilisers contain compounds of nitrogen (N), phosphorus (P) and potassium (K) in different proportions. They provide the essential elements needed by crops for growth and are used to improve agricultural productivity.

NPK fertilisers are made with ammonia produced in the Haber process.

Making Fertiliser in the Laboratory

Ammonium salts used to make fertilisers can be prepared in the laboratory by reacting ammonia solution with different acids:

- Ammonia + Nitric acid ➡ Ammonium nitrate
- Ammonia + Sulfuric acid ➡ Ammonium sulfate
- Ammonia + Phosphoric acid ➡ Ammonium phosphate

Each reaction is a neutralisation reaction that can be performed as a titration, which uses an indicator to show when all the ammonia solution has reacted.

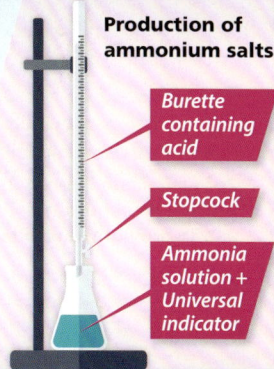

Production of ammonium salts

Burette containing acid

Stopcock

Ammonia solution + Universal indicator

Industrial Production of Fertiliser

In industry, ammonium nitrate is produced by reacting ammonia and nitric acid in large vats at high concentrations.

Potassium chloride, potassium sulfate and phosphate rock are obtained by mining. However, phosphate rock must be treated before it can be used as a fertiliser because it is insoluble. Therefore, it is treated with nitric, sulfuric or phosphoric acid to produce soluble salts suitable for fertilisers.

Acid Added	Production
Nitric acid	Phosphate rock and nitric acid produces phosphoric acid and calcium nitrate. The phosphoric acid is then reacted with ammonia to produce ammonium phosphate.
Sulfuric acid	Phosphate rock and sulfuric acid produce single superphosphate, a mixture of calcium phosphate and calcium sulfate.
Phosphoric acid	Phosphate rock and phosphoric acid produce triple superphosphate, or calcium phosphate.

Potassium chloride and potassium sulfate are soluble in water, so they can be easily separated from impurities once mined.

daydream
EDUCATION

Applications of Science

Scientific developments have led to remarkable discoveries and innovations. However, they have also created issues related to social, economic, environmental and ethical factors. Therefore, the evaluation of scientific applications should consider the advantages and disadvantages related to these issues.

Example: Evaluate the use of zoos to breed animals.

When evaluating something, always remember to consider the arguments for and against.

Social

How do zoos affect people?

- Zoos stimulate interest in animals and provide an opportunity to educate people and to promote animal protection.
- Animals can escape.

Economic

How do zoos affect the economy?

- Zoos create jobs and support local businesses.
- Some zoos donate money to animal charities.
- Zoos can be expensive to run and maintain.

Environmental

How do zoos affect the environment?

- Zoos provide a home for animals that have had their habitats destroyed.
- Removing animals from the wild can further endanger the wild population.

Ethical

Are zoos ethical?

- Zoos save endangered species and can help breed endangered species.
- It is cruel to keep animals in captivity.
- Surplus animals are sometimes killed.

Personal: How do zoos affect you? Do zoos affect your life in a positive or negative way?

It is not always possible to answer questions relating to scientific developments, especially ethical questions. This is particularly difficult when there is little or no existing data. Sometimes it can take years of research for new data to come to light.

For example, for years, diesel was promoted as a way of reducing CO_2 emissions. However, in 2012, studies by the European Environment Agency found evidence that nitrogen dioxide ($NO2$) from diesel fumes were very harmful to human health, causing thousands of premature deaths each year. As a result, there has been a push to phase out diesel cars.

daydream EDUCATION

Peer Review

Peer review is a process that involves the evaluation of scientific, academic or professional work by others working in the same field.

Scientists publish their results in scientific journals. Before a work is published, its validity is checked by experts – this is peer review.

Scientific journals are print and online magazines that contain articles written by scientists about their research.

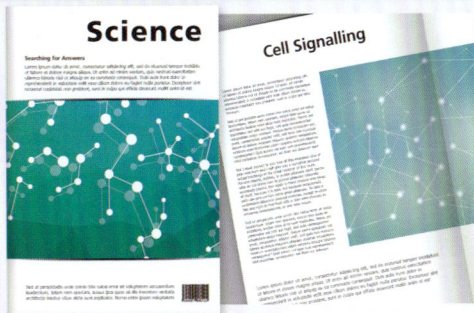

Science

Searching for Answers

Cell Signalling

Publication can lead to collaborations between scientists to develop ideas or inspire new ones.

It is important that experts review research in journals. Peer review lets readers know that they can be confident that the claims made are valid and believable. However, this does not mean the research findings are correct, just that they are not obviously wrong.

The Peer Review Process

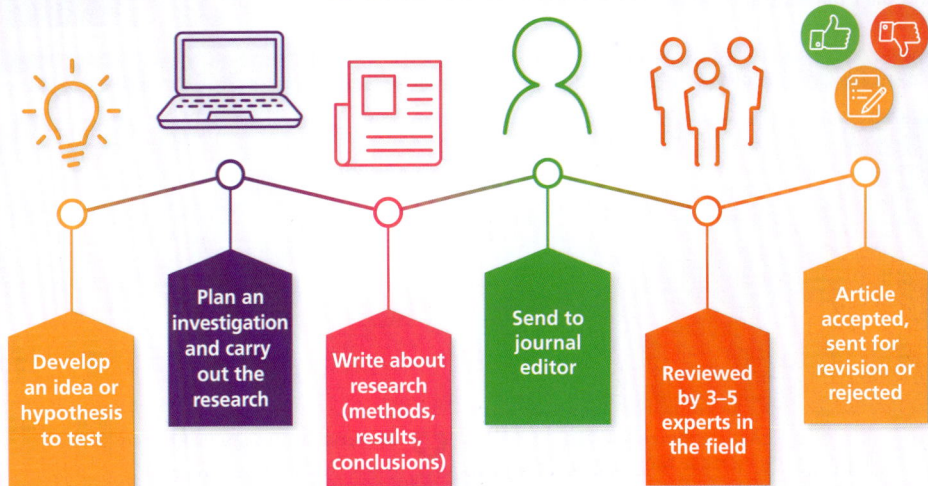

Develop an idea or hypothesis to test	Plan an investigation and carry out the research	Write about research (methods, results, conclusions)	Send to journal editor	Reviewed by 3–5 experts in the field	Article accepted, sent for revision or rejected

Beware!

Scientific reports in the media do not go through peer review so they may be inaccurate or biased. If the report is based on a journal article, get more reliable information by reading the conclusions of the research.

Risk

*A **hazard** is anything that can cause harm.*
***Risk** is the likelihood of a hazard causing harm.*

Measuring Risk

The size of risk posed by something depends on how hazardous (harmful) it is and the likelihood of it happening. Look at the example below:

Lightning is ***very hazardous*** – it can kill.
But the ***likelihood*** of being hit by lightning is ***very low***.
Therefore, the risk of being killed by lightning is low.

Hazards & Risk in Science

There are various hazards in practical science. It is important to identify these hazards and to try to reduce their risk and the likelihood of them occurring and causing harm.

Although scientific or technological developments frequently bring about many benefits, they can also often introduce new risks.

For example, the development of e-cigarettes has helped significantly increase the number of people giving up smoking. However, scientists are still unsure whether the chemicals used in the cigarettes are harmful to the body.

Look at the two examples below. Are the benefits of these technologies worth the risk?

Genetic Engineering

+ Benefit: Genetic engineering can significantly increase food production.

– Risk: There are serious concerns about the effects of genetically modified foods on human health and biodiversity. Also, gene transfer between plants may lead to an uncontrollable 'escape' of genes into wild plants.

X-Rays

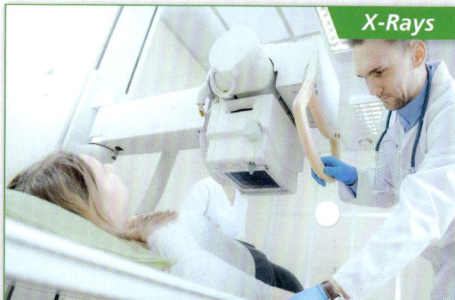

+ Benefit: X-rays are used to check for bone fractures.

– Risk: Radiation exposure can cause cell mutations that may lead to cancer. However, this risk is thought to be very low.

daydream EDUCATION

The size of risk posed by a hazard can be measured by looking at the number of times the hazard caused harm in a sample. Look at the example below:

Deaths per 1 billion passenger miles

Motorcycle	212.57
Car	7.28

The statistics above show that travelling by motorcycle is riskier than travelling by car.

Perceived Risk vs Measured Risk

The perception of risk is often very different from measured risk.

Familiar vs Unfamiliar

Which has the higher risk?

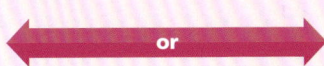

Running a marathon

or

Parachuting out of a plane

Although most people think parachuting out of a plane is riskier than running a marathon, the risk of dying in both activities is roughly the same: eight in one million. This is because familiar things feel less risky than unfamiliar things.

Visible vs Invisible

Some 3.8 million premature deaths are annually attributed to air pollution. However, because air pollution is invisible, people tend to underestimate its risk. This is the same for many other invisible hazards.

A similar perception applies to hazards that take a long time to take effect, such as an unhealthy diet.

Imposed vs Voluntary

Around 200 years ago, the leading cause of death was communicable diseases caused by poor sanitation and living conditions. People usually did not have a choice about this – the risks were imposed.

Now, the leading cause of death is non-communicable diseases like heart disease and cancer. Often, the risk of these is increased by lifestyle choices, or voluntary risks.

In general, people are more likely to accept the risks that are within their control than the risks over which they have no control.

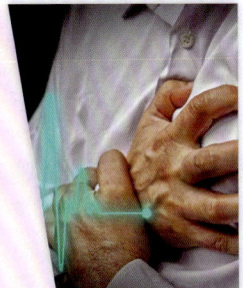

Apparatus

Scientific apparatus are specialist instruments that are used during experiments. During experiments, it is important to use the correct apparatus, wear the appropriate protective equipment and understand the hazards involved.

Experimental Apparatus

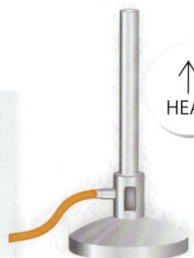

Bunsen Burner
A heating apparatus used in laboratories

Conical Flask
Used for heating and collecting solutions

Filter Paper & Funnel
Used for separating solids from liquids

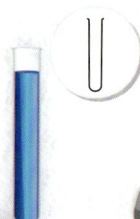

Test Tubes
Used for heating and testing small quantities of solids and liquids

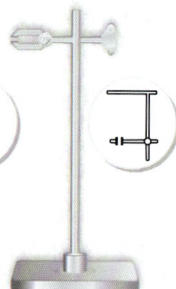

Clamp Stand
Used to safely hold apparatus in position

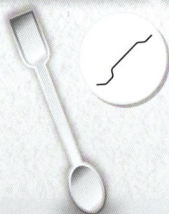

Spatula
Used to handle solids and transfer them from containers

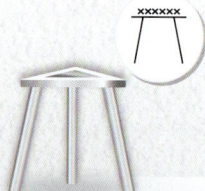

Tripod & Gauze
Used to support apparatus above a Bunsen burner

Beaker
Used for stirring, mixing and heating liquids

Evaporating Dish
Used to heat and evaporate liquids

Measuring Apparatus

Measuring Cylinder
Volume – cm^3, dm^3, ml, l

Stopwatch
Time – s, min

Newtonmeter/Forcemeter
Force – N

Thermometer
Temperature – °C

daydream
EDUCATION

Hazards

A hazard is something that poses a risk and that could potentially cause harm. Hazard symbols are used on containers to indicate the dangers associated with the contents and to inform people about how to use the substance safely.

 **Explosive**

 **Flammable**

 **Oxidising**

 **Corrosive**

 **Toxic**

 **Health hazard**

Safety

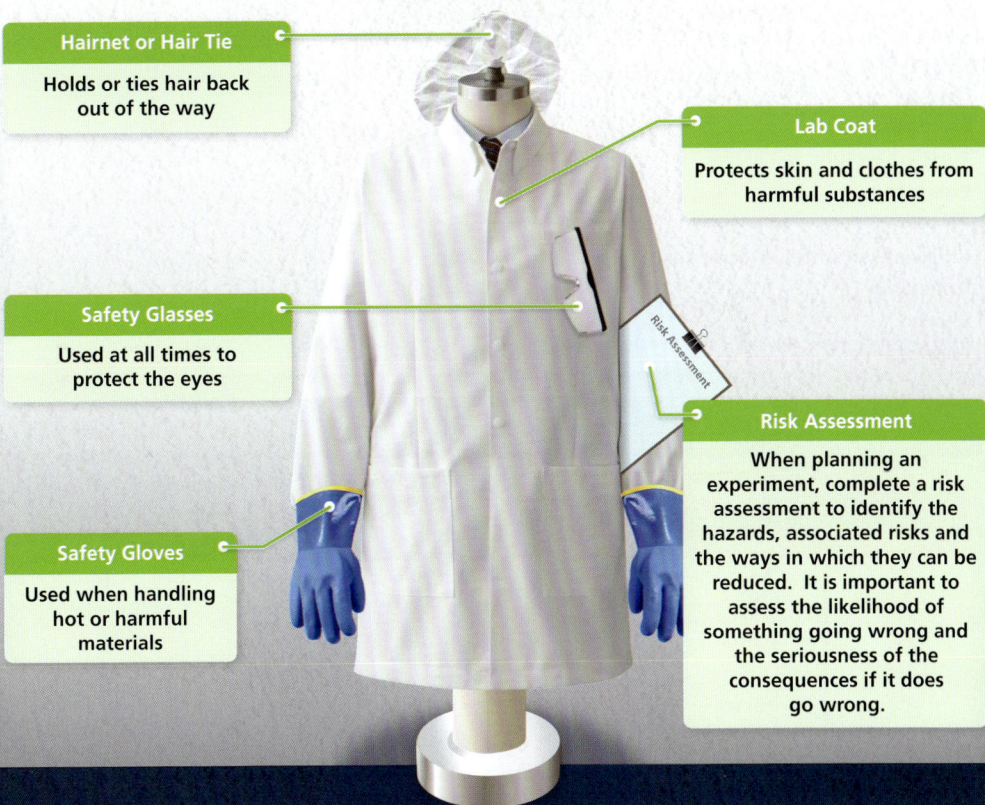

Hairnet or Hair Tie

Holds or ties hair back out of the way

Lab Coat

Protects skin and clothes from harmful substances

Safety Glasses

Used at all times to protect the eyes

Safety Gloves

Used when handling hot or harmful materials

Risk Assessment

When planning an experiment, complete a risk assessment to identify the hazards, associated risks and the ways in which they can be reduced. It is important to assess the likelihood of something going wrong and the seriousness of the consequences if it does go wrong.

daydream EDUCATION

Physical Units

International System of Units (SI Units)

Quantity Name	Unit Name	Unit Symbol
Length	metre	m
Mass	kilogram	kg
Time	second	s
Electric current	ampere	A
Thermodynamic temperature	kelvin	K
Amount of substance	mole	mol
Luminous intensity	candela	cd

Other Units

Quantity Name	Unit Name	Unit Symbol
Temperature	degree Celsius	°C
Energy	joule	J
Frequency	hertz	Hz
Force or weight	newton	N
Pressure	pascal	Pa
Power	watt	W
Voltage (potential difference)	volt	V
Resistance	ohm	Ω
Charge	coulomb	C
Capacitance	farad	F

SI Prefixes

These are added to unit names to produce multiples and sub-multiples, or fractions, of the original unit.

Multiples

Factor	Name	Symbol
10^{12}	tera	T
10^{9}	giga	G
10^{6}	mega	M
10^{3}	kilo	k
10^{2}	hecto	h
10^{1}	deca	da

Fractions

Factor	Name	Symbol
10^{-12}	pico	p
10^{-9}	nano	n
10^{-6}	micro	µ
10^{-3}	milli	m
10^{-2}	centi	c
10^{-1}	deci	d

Examples

You need to be able to convert from one unit to another.

10^{3} m (1,000 m) = 1 km 10^{3} g (1,000 g) = 1 kg 10^{-2} m (0.01 m) = 1 cm 10^{-3} g (0.001 g) = 1 mg

daydream EDUCATION

Planning

A good plan is well designed for its purpose.

Reasons to Plan an Investigation

Make Observations
What structures can be seen in cells?

Produce a Substance
How can a salt be made using neutralisation?

Test a Hypothesis
Is the extension of a spring proportional to the weight added?

Explore Phenomenon
What are wave patterns like in oceans across the world?

What to Think About When Planning

What data or observations need to be collected? ▶ How many measurements need to be taken to see a pattern? ▶ What range of measurements is needed? ▶ How many repeats is enough?	I need to measure the extension of the spring as the mass on the end changes. I will increase the mass by 10 g (0.1 N) until 100 g (1 N) is reached. I will repeat the experiment twice.
What apparatus and techniques should be used?	I will use a spring held on a clamp stand, a 50-cm ruler and slotted masses. I will measure extension by viewing the spring at eye level and taking the reading from the bottom of the spring.
How is the apparatus used to record accurate measurements?	I will attach the ruler to the clamp stand to make sure it is measuring the length of the spring accurately.
What are the possible hazards? How can the risk of harm be reduced?	The clamp stand could fall over. Therefore, I will attach the clamp stand to the table with a clamp and make sure it is not placed over my feet.
What are the variables?	Independent variable = mass Dependent variable = length of extension

Variables

Investigations are often performed to identify if there are patterns or relationships between two variables. One variable is changed to see how it affects another variable.

Independent Variable
The independent variable is the one that is changed.

Dependent Variable
The dependent variable is the one that is measured for each change in the independent variable; it's what the investigator thinks will be affected during the experiment.

Control Variables
Control variables are all the other variables in an investigation that should be kept the same to ensure that it is the independent variable that is causing the dependent variable to change.

daydream EDUCATION

Presenting Data

Presenting data in an appropriate way makes it easy to spot patterns and draw conclusions from results.

Categorical Data

Includes non-numerical data (e.g. colour) and numerical data with definite values (e.g. number of cells)

Continuous Data

Numerical data that can take any value (e.g. height or time)

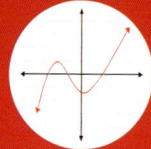

A population of plants is found growing in a field, including in a shady area under a tree.

There is lots of data that can be measured to answer the question:

How do light and shade affect plant growth?

Graphing Rules

- Label both axes.

- Give your charts and graphs a title.

- Include a key if you have more than one set of data.

- Usually, the dependent variable goes on the y-axis and the independent variable on the x-axis.

Bar Charts

Bar charts are used to present categorical data. Bar charts help to compare data.

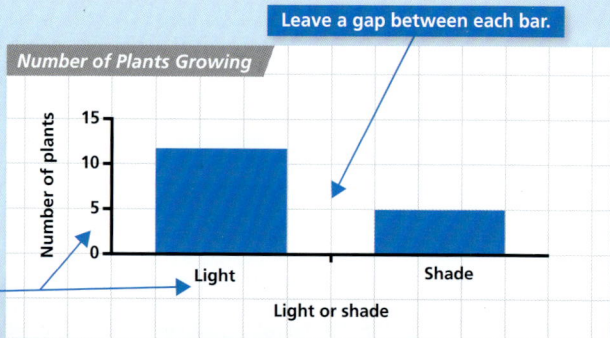

Leave a gap between each bar.

Number of Plants Growing

Number of plants

15

10

5

0

Light

Shade

Light or shade

Use equal intervals on both axes.

daydream EDUCATION

Line Graph

Line graphs are used to display continuous data. They can be used to show trends and change over time.

Change over Time

Plant Height over Time

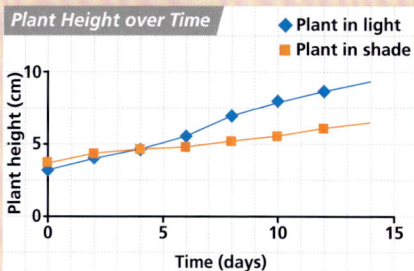

- ◆ Plant in light
- ■ Plant in shade

Data is plotted as a series of points that are joined by straight lines.

A Trend

How Light Intensity Affects Mean Leaf Area

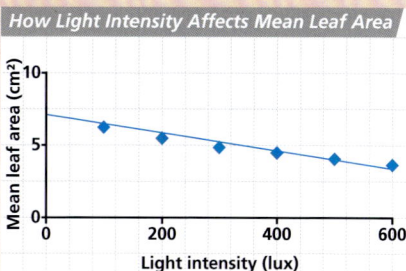

A line of best fit can be drawn to show an overall trend and that a proportional relationship exists between the two variables. In this example, as light intensity increases, mean leaf area decreases.

Frequency Tables and Charts

A frequency table is used to record how often a value (or set of values) occurs.

Length of Top Leaf (cm)	Frequency	
	Plants in Shade	Plants in Light
$3.0 \leq l < 3.5$	2	3
$3.5 \leq l < 4.0$	5	7
$4.0 \leq l < 4.5$	4	5
$4.5 \leq l < 5.0$	7	6
$5.0 \leq l < 5.5$	7	4
Total	**25**	**25**

Data from frequency tables is often displayed in frequency charts.

How Light Intensity Affects Leaf Length

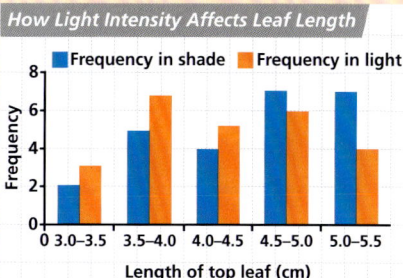

- ■ Frequency in shade
- ■ Frequency in light

The groups (intervals) must be the same. Make sure to include units of measure in the column headings. A sample of 25 plants from each environment was used. The interval $5.0 \leq l < 5.5$ is equal to or greater than 5.0 and less than 5.5.

daydream EDUCATION

Evaluating Data

Students performed an experiment to determine how temperature affects reaction rate. They measured the time taken for a certain amount of sulfur to form when sodium thiosulfate solution reacts with acid at different temperatures.

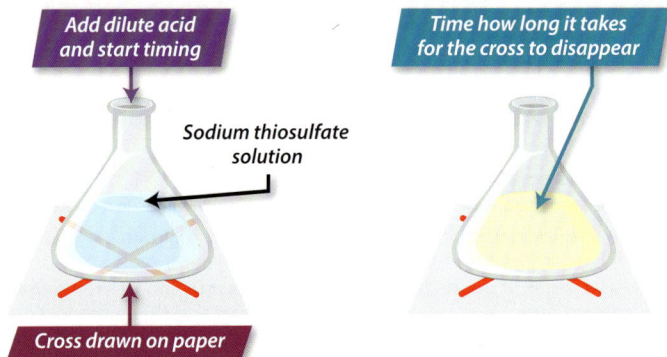

Add dilute acid and start timing

Time how long it takes for the cross to disappear

Sodium thiosulfate solution

Cross drawn on paper

This was measured by determining how long it took for the solution to become completely opaque at different temperatures.

Temperature (°C)	Time for Cross to Disappear (s)		
	1	2	3
10	196	194	196
20	95	88	96
30	53	53	53
40	28	24	26

Precision

Measurements are precise if they are similar and cluster around a single value.

How to Check for Precision: Look how close the repeated values are.

Evaluation: At 30°C, the repeats are all the same, which means these results are very precise. The results at 40°C are not as precise because they have a range of 4 seconds.

Range: the difference between the lowest and highest measurements

daydream EDUCATION

Accuracy

An accurate measurement is one that is close to the true value. There are few errors and little uncertainty.

How to Check for Accuracy:

Errors: Random errors are shown by anomalous (odd-looking) results, but they can be reduced by taking more measurements and finding the mean value.

Systematic errors are difficult to spot from results, so the equipment should be checked. Any anomalies should be investigated to try and find the cause and, if due to error, should be discarded.

Random error: results varying in unpredictable ways

Systematic error: measurements that differ from the true value by a consistent amount every time; usually caused by a problem with the measuring equipment

Mean

The sum of values divided by the number of values

Example for 40°C: $\frac{28 + 24 + 26}{3} = 26$

Percentage Uncertainty

$\frac{range}{mean} \times 100$

Example for 40°C: $\frac{4}{26} \times 100 = 15.38$

Uncertainty: The range of measurements around the mean. A low uncertainty is a sign of high accuracy.

Evaluation: The second recorded value at 20°C (88 s) is an anomaly (probably due to a mistake in measurement). The uncertainty is highest for 40°C because these show the most variation around the mean.

Repeatability

Measurements are considered repeatable if they produce similar results when performed by the same investigator under the same conditions.

How to Check for Repeatability:
Look how close the repeats are. In the experiment above, the measurements show good repeatability because the overall measurements are around the same for each repeated value.

Reproducibility

Measurements are considered reproducible if they produce similar results when performed by a different investigator with different equipment.

How to Check for Reproducibility:
Get someone else to carry out the experiment using different equipment. If their experiment produces similar results to yours, the measurements can be considered reproducible.

daydream EDUCATION

Standard Form

Standard form, or standard index form, is used when writing very small or very large numbers.

In standard form, a number is always written in the following format:

A is always a number between 1 and 10: $1 \leq A < 10$	$A \times 10^{n}$	***n* tells you how many places you need to move the decimal point.**

Converting Numbers into Standard Form

When writing large numbers in standard form, *n* is always positive.				
$8,000,000$	$=$	$8 \times 1,000,000$	$=$	8×10^{6}
$45,000,000$	$=$	$4.5 \times 10,000,000$	$=$	4.5×10^{7}
$160,000$	$=$	$1.6 \times 100,000$	$=$	1.6×10^{5}

When writing small numbers in standard form, *n* is always negative.				
0.000465	$=$	$4.65 \div 10,000$	$=$	4.65×10^{-4}
0.009	$=$	$9 \div 1,000$	$=$	9.0×10^{-3}
0.0000077	$=$	$7.7 \div 1,000,000$	$=$	7.7×10^{-6}

Examples

Example 1

There are around 87,000,000 species on the Earth. Convert this to standard form.

$$87,000,000 = 8.7 \times 10,000,000 = 8.7 \times 10^{7}$$

The decimal point has moved seven places to the left:

$$8.7000000$$
$$7\ 6\ 5\ 4\ 3\ 2\ 1$$

Example 2

The diameter of the DNA helix is 0.000000002 m. Convert this to standard form.

$$0.000000002 = 2.0 \div 1,000,000,000 = 2 \times 10^{-9}$$

The decimal point has moved nine places to the right:

$$0000000002.0$$
$$1\ 2\ 3\ 4\ 5\ 6\ 7\ 8\ 9$$

daydream EDUCATION

Rounding to Significant Figures

Significant Figures

If something is 'significant', it is large or important.
Therefore, 'most significant' means 'largest' or 'most important'.

In the number 169.2, the most significant figure is 1 because it has the largest value, 100.	Hundreds	Tens	Ones		Tenths
	1	**6**	**9**	**•**	**2**

The first significant figure in a number is the first digit that is not zero. Any leading zeros are insignificant (placeholders).	0302.14 00.507 0.00621

Rounding to Significant Figures

To round to significant figures, identify the significant figure that is being rounded to and round as normal.

The density of iron is 7.874 g/cm³. To round 7.874 to 2 significant figures:

1	Identify the second significant figure.	7.874
2	Look at the digit to the right of the one that is being rounded. It is more than 5 so round up.	7.874
3	When rounding decimals, there is no need to add zeros after the significant figures.	7.9

7.874 rounded to 2 significant figures is 7.9.

An object has a mass of 0.046748 g. To round 0.046748 to 3 significant figures:

1	Identify the third significant figure.	0.046748
2	Look at the digit to the right of the one that is being rounded. It is less than 5 so leave it alone.	0.046748
3	When rounding decimals, there is no need to add zeros after the significant figures.	0.0467

0.046748 rounded to 3 significant figures is 0.0467.

Taylor ran 400 metres in 52 seconds. Calculate her speed to 2 significant figures.

1	Calculate Taylor's speed: speed = $\dfrac{distance}{time}$ = $\dfrac{400}{52}$ = 7.692307692 m/s	
2	Identify the second significant figure.	7.692307692
3	Look at the digit to the right of the one that is being rounded. It is more than 5 so round up.	7.692307692
4	When rounding decimals, there is no need to add zeros after the significant figures.	7.7

Taylor's speed to 2 significant figures was 7.7 m/s.

Sampling

It is not always possible to collect information on a whole population. In such instances, a proportion (sample) of the population is used.

Ecologists use a wide range of sampling methods to determine the abundance and distribution of species in an ecosystem.

A larger sample will more accurately reflect the population. A sample that is too small is likely to lead to statistical bias.

Quadrats

A quadrat is a square frame of a specific size (often 0.5×0.5 m). It is used to sample an area that is too big to completely survey. The number of one or more species in each quadrat is counted and then scaled up to estimate the number in the whole area.

It would be nearly impossible to count the whole population of daisy plants in a field, but this can be estimated by using quadrats.

Quadrat Example

1	Measure the area of the field.	40 m × 30 m = 1,200 m²
2	Identify how many quadrats are required to provide a sufficient sample area, and calculate the total area.	20 quadrats: 20 × 0.25 m² = 5 m²
3	Place the quadrats in random locations, and count the total number of daisies in each quadrat.	In total, 86 daisies were found in the 20 quadrats.
4	Divide the total area of the field by the area surveyed to identify how much bigger the field is than the survey area.	1,200 ÷ 5 = 240
5	The field is 240 times bigger than the area surveyed. To find an estimate of the total number of daisies in the field, multiply the number of daisies found in all the quadrats by 240.	86 × 240 = 20,640

The accuracy of this estimate can be increased by taking more samples.

Transects

A transect is a line that is used to measure the distribution of organisms, not their numbers. It is usually marked by a rope or tape measure.

Samples are taken at regular intervals along the line, and the species seen at each point are recorded. The line is usually laid along some sort of gradient (e.g. low-tide mark to high-tide mark) to see its effect on distribution.

daydream EDUCATION

Averages

An average is a measure of the middle value of a data set. There are three main types of averages: mean, mode and median.

Mean

The mean is the sum of the values divided by the number of values.

$$\text{mean} = \frac{\text{sum of values}}{\text{number of values}}$$

Abbie is measuring her reaction time using the ruler drop test:

Attempt	1	2	3	4	5	6	7	8	9	10
Distance (cm)	19.5	18	12	16	12	10.6	7.5	8	6.4	7

$$\text{Mean} = \frac{19.5 + 18 + 12 + 16 + 12 + 10.6 + 7.5 + 8 + 6.4 + 7}{10} = \frac{117}{10} = 11.7 \text{ cm}$$

Mode

The mode is the value that occurs most often.

The mode for Abbie's results was 12 cm. It occurred twice, in her third and fifth attempts.

Median

The median is the middle value when the data is arranged in order of size.

Attempt	9	10	7	8	6	3	5	4	2	1
Distance (cm)	6.4	7	7.5	8	10.6	12	12	16	18	19.5

As there is an even number of values, the median is the mean of the middle two values.

$$\text{Median} = \frac{10.6 + 12}{2} = \frac{22.6}{2} = 11.3 \text{ cm}$$

Range

The range is the difference between the lowest value and the highest value in a data set.

Attempt 9 6.4 ← **Range = 13.1** → **Attempt 1** 19.5

To find the range, subtract the lowest value from the highest value. The range of Abbie's results is 13.1 cm.

Scatter Graphs

Scatter graphs are used to show how closely two sets of data are related. Correlation describes how the two sets of data are related.

Positive Correlation

When the **plotted points** go upward from left to right, there is **positive correlation**.

As one quantity increases, the other increases. As one quantity decreases, the other decreases.

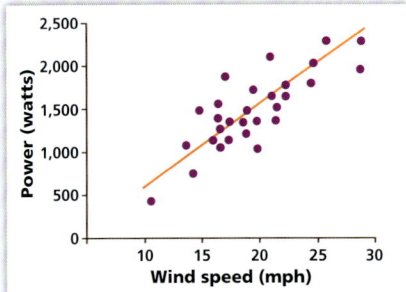

This graph shows that there is positive correlation between wind speed and the amount of electricity generated by a wind turbine. As the speed of a wind turbine increases, so does the amount of electricity generated.

Negative Correlation

When the **plotted points** go downward from left to right, there is **negative correlation**.

As one quantity increases, the other decreases.

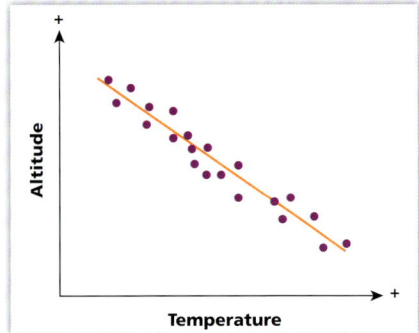

This graph shows that there is **negative correlation** between altitude and temperature. As altitude increases, temperature decreases.

No Correlation

When there is no linear relationship between two data sets, there is **no correlation**.

This graph shows that the number of children that a person has is not related to his/her average daily sugar consumption.

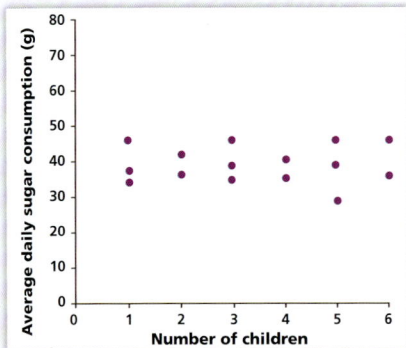

Line of Best Fit

A **line of best fit** is a line that is drawn through the centre of a group of data points.

When the plotted points are close to the **line of best fit**, there is **strong correlation**. When they are spread out on either side of the **line of best fit**, there is **moderate correlation**.

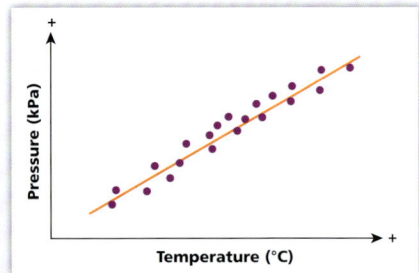

This graph shows a **strong positive correlation**.

Correlation and Causation

A correlation between two variables does not necessarily mean there is a direct cause-and-effect relationship between them.

Example >>> There is a strong positive correlation between germ exposure and disease development. However, these variables are not directly related. Germs alone do not cause disease. The causative factor is a compromised immune system.

daydream EDUCATION

Rearranging Formulae

A formula is an equation that shows the relationship between different variables.

Sometimes you can rearrange formulae by using inverse operations to make them easier to work with and solve. In the examples below, the equations have been rearranged to make x the subject:

$$x - 4 = 9$$
$$+4 \quad +4$$
$$x = 13$$

Addition and **subtraction** are inverse operations.

$$x + 7 = 12$$
$$-7 \quad -7$$
$$x = 5$$

$$mx = t$$
$$\div m \quad \div m$$
$$x = \frac{t}{m}$$

Multiplication and **division** are inverse operations.

$$\frac{x}{r} = 12$$
$$\times r \quad \times r$$
$$x = 12r$$

$$x^2 = w$$
$$\sqrt{} \quad \sqrt{}$$
$$x = \pm\sqrt{w}$$

Finding the **square root** of a number is the inverse operation of **squaring** that number.

Square

$$\sqrt{x} = a$$
$$2 \quad 2$$
$$x = a^2$$

You can rearrange the formula for speed to make distance or time the subject.

$$\text{speed} = \frac{\text{distance}}{\text{time}}$$

Light travels at an approximate speed of 300,000 km/s. The Earth orbits the Sun at a distance of just under 150 million km.

How long does it take for sunlight to reach the Earth?

1

Rearrange the formula so **time** is the subject.

$$s = \frac{d}{t}$$
$$\times t \quad \times t$$
$$s \times t = d$$
$$\div s \quad \div s$$
$$t = \frac{d}{s}$$

2

Substitute the known values into the formula and solve.

$$t = \frac{150,000,000}{300,000}$$
$$t = 500 \text{ s}$$
$$t = 8 \text{ minutes } 20 \text{ seconds}$$

You can rearrange the formula for wave speed to make frequency or wavelength the subject.

wave speed = frequency × wavelength

The water waves in a ripple tank have a speed of 0.31 m/s and a wavelength of 1.6 cm.

What is the frequency of the water waves?

1

Rearrange the formula so **frequency** is the subject.

wave speed = frequency × wavelength

$\div$ wavelength $\qquad$ $\div$ wavelength

$$\text{frequency} = \frac{\text{wave speed}}{\text{wavelength}}$$

2

Convert the measurement for wavelength from cm to m as wavespeed is measured in m/s. Then, substitute the known values into the formula and solve.

$$1.6 \text{ cm} = 0.016 \text{ m}$$
$$\text{frequency} = \frac{0.31}{0.016}$$
$$\text{frequency} = 19.4 \text{ m/s (3 s.f.)}$$

Substitution

When substituting in sport, one player is swapped for another. The same principle applies to formulae in science: variables (letters) are swapped with values.

Calculate the potential difference across the battery in the following circuit:

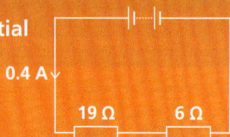

0.4 A

19 Ω   6 Ω

potential difference = current × resistance

1 Calculate total resistance.

19 + 6 = 25 Ω

2 Substitute the known numbers into the formula.

potential difference = 0.4 × 25

3 Follow the rules of BIDMAS to find the answer.

potential difference = 10 V

Calculate the relative formula mass (M_r) of sulfuric acid.

The relative atomic masses (A_r) needed for this equation are: hydrogen = 1, sulfur = 32, oxygen = 16.

H_2SO_4

1 Write out the formula with the number of atoms.

(2 × H) + (1 × S) + (4 × O)

2 Substitute the relative atomic masses into the formula.

(2 × 1) + (1 × 32) + (4 × 16)

3 Follow the rules of BIDMAS to find the answer.

2 + 32 + 64 = 98

Matt is measuring his reaction time by using the ruler drop test. The mean distance his ruler dropped is 14.2 cm. Calculate Matt's mean reaction time (in seconds).

$$\text{reaction time} = \sqrt{\frac{\text{mean drop distance}}{490}}$$

1 Substitute the known numbers into the formula.

$$\text{reaction time} = \sqrt{\frac{14.2}{490}}$$

2 Follow the rules of BIDMAS to find the answer.

reaction time = 0.17 s (2 s.f.)

daydream
EDUCATION

Straight Line Graphs

A straight line graph represents a linear relationship, where an increase or decrease in one variable causes a corresponding increase or decrease in the other variable.

Straight Line Equation

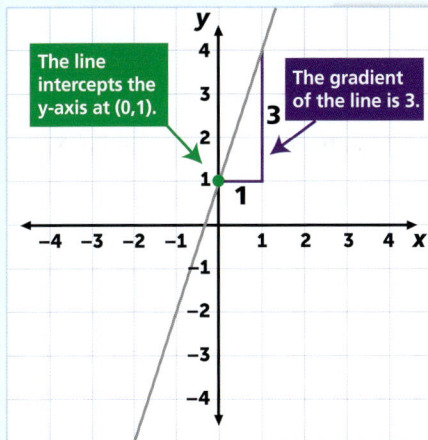

The line intercepts the y-axis at (0,1).

The gradient of the line is 3.

The standard equation of a straight line is:

$$y = mx + c$$

m = gradient of line c = y-intercept

y-intercept = where the line passes through the y-axis

The gradient can be calculated by using the formula:

$$\text{gradient } (m) = \frac{\text{change in } y}{\text{change in } x}$$

The equation of the straight line is: $y = 3x + 1$

$$\text{gradient } (m) = \frac{\text{change in } y}{\text{change in } x} = \frac{3}{1} = 3$$

y-intercept = (0,1)

Finding the Equation of a Straight Line

To find the equation of a straight line, follow the steps outlined below:

1 Find the y-intercept of the graph. This is the value of *c*. The line intercepts the y-axis at **(0,1)** so c = **+1**.

2 Pick two sets of coordinates on the line, and use the following formula to calculate the gradient (*m*):

$$m = \frac{\text{change in } y}{\text{change in } x}$$
$$= \frac{-1 - -3}{1 - 2}$$
$$= \frac{2}{-1}$$
$$m = -2$$

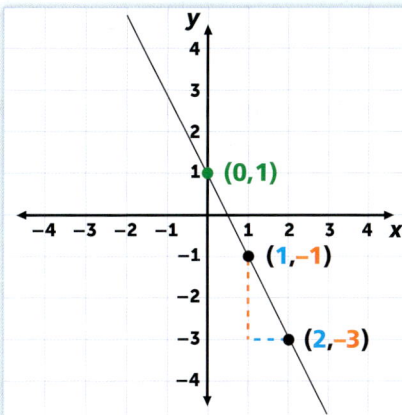

(0,1)

(1,–1)

(2,–3)

The gradient (*m*) is –2 and the intercept (*c*) is +1. Therefore, the equation of the line is:

$$y = -2x + 1$$

daydream
EDUCATION

Area, Volume & Surface Area

Area — Area is the total size of a flat surface.

Rectangle/Square

What is the area of the football field?

70 m
100 m

Area of rectangle = **length** × **width**
= **100** × **70**
Area of field = **7,000 m²**

Triangle

What is the area of the sign?

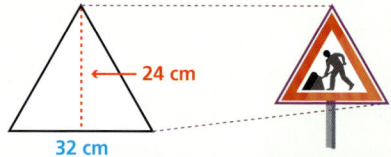

24 cm
32 cm

Area of triangle = $\frac{1}{2}$ × **base** × **height**
= $\frac{1}{2}$ × **32** × **24**
Area of sign = **384 cm²**

Volume — Volume is the amount of space inside a 3D shape or object.

Prisms & Cylinders

Volume of prism or cylinder = cross-sectional area × length

Prisms and cylinders are solid objects that maintain a constant cross-sectional area along their length.

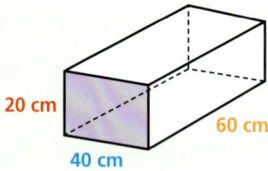

20 cm 60 cm 40 cm

$V = w \times h \times l$
= $40 \times 20 \times 60$
= **48,000 cm³**

1.5 m 3.5 m 2 m

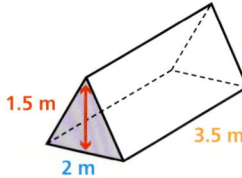

$V = \frac{1}{2} \times b \times h \times l$
= $\frac{1}{2} \times 2 \times 1.5 \times 3.5$
= **5.25 m³**

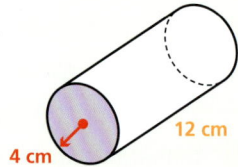

4 cm 12 cm

$V = \pi r^2 \times l$
= $\pi \times 16 \times 12$
= **603.19 cm³ (2 d.p.)**

Surface Area

Surface area is the total area of the outer surface of a 3D object. The surface area of a solid figure is equal to the total area of its net. To calculate the surface area of a shape, work out the area of each face and add them together.

Net

2 cm
6 cm
2 cm
2 cm 3 cm 3 cm
3 cm

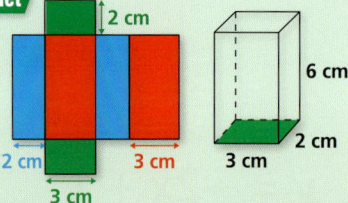

Calculate the areas of the different sized faces.

Area = $l \times w$
= 3×6
= **18 cm²**

Area = $l \times w$
= 2×6
= **12 cm²**

Area = $l \times w$
= 3×2
= **6 cm²**

Multiply these areas by the number of corresponding faces.

18 × 2 = **36 cm²** | 12 × 2 = **24 cm²** | 6 × 2 = **12 cm²**

Add the areas together: 36 + 24 + 12 = **72 cm²**

daydream EDUCATION

Notes

Notes

Index

Index